VICTORY
IN JESUS

VICTORY
IN JESUS

Running the Race
You Are Meant to Win

E.V. HILL

MOODY PUBLISHERS

CHICAGO

Editorial services by:
Julie-Allyson Ieron, Joy Media

Library of Congress Cataloging-in-Publication Data

Hill, E. V. (Edward Victor), 1933-2003
  Victory in Jesus: running the race you are meant to win/E. V. Hill.
     p.cm.
  ISBN 0-8024-3133-X
  1. Christian Life—Baptist authors. I. Title.
  BV4501.3.H54 2003
  248.4'861—dc21

2003005530

1 3 5 7 9 10 8 6 4 2

Printed in the United States of America

CONTENTS

Introduction   7

1. You Must Be Born Again—Matthew 16:16   9

2. How to Rejoice Always—Philippians 4:4   15

3. How to Escape Depression— Matthew 11:28   23

4. Why the Struggle?—Job 23:10   33

5. The Experience of a Dry Brook—James 5:17–18   41

6. Courage to Face Tomorrow . . . Because of What God Did Yesterday—1 Samuel 17:37   49

7. If the Foundations Be Destroyed—Psalm 11:3   57

8. The Model Prayer—Matthew 6:9-13   69

9. The Power of God—Isaiah 40:29–31   79

10. The Burden of the Lord—John 3:16   89

11. The Big One—1 Thessalonians 4:16-17   97

Appendix 1: A Memorial Message—Job 1:21   105

Appendix 2: A Biographical Sketch of Dr. Hill   111

Epilogue   117

INTRODUCTION

Two years ago, Moody Publishers jumped at the opportunity to publish Dr. E.V. Hill's first two books. This counselor of presidents and mighty preacher of God was ready to have his sermons committed to writing, and we were ready. We are grateful to Joe Mines and It's Like Fire Ministries for making this publishing connection.

Pastors Hill's association with the Moody Bible Institute went back decades. His preaching at various Moody sponsored conferences stirred the hearts of eager listeners. He brought a rare combination of unashamed proclamation of the whole of Scripture and powerful, often personal application points. Even more, his delivery was unforgettable! No wonder Time Magazine named him one the top seven preachers in the United States.

For this reason, we were pleased in 2002 to release Dr. Hill's first book *A Savior Worth Having*. This collection of sermons all centered around his favorite subject, Jesus Christ. We even included a limited edition CD containing his Moody Founder's Week message from February 1980, "What You Have When You Have Jesus."

This second book contains messages about the next steps in the Christian life. Wonderfully practical subjects like courage, joy, prayer, and struggle. "The Power of God," chapter 9, addresses the much debated subject of the social gospel. And you'll want to make sure that before closing the book, you know what the burden of God is all about (chapter 10). A reviewer predicts: "Readers will lose themselves in Hill's dynamic and fiery writing."

The first typeset pages of this book dated February 5, 2003, never made it to Dr. Hill for approval. At that point, he was well into his final battle for life. And on February 24, God called E.V. Hill home.

We debated about whether we should proceed with the book. And if so, should we include the appendix with his very moving message delivered at his wife's memorial service, as we had planned? After consulting with his close associate and other family members, we decided to publish *Victory in Jesus: Running the Race You Are Meant to Win.* We did add a final epilogue, the obituary used earlier this year at Pastor Hill's funeral service.

Dr. E.V. Hill now knows personally the reality of his closing words from Jane Edna's memorial service:

In 1 Corinthians 15:52 Paul says, "In a moment, in the twinkling of an eye, at the last trump: for the trumpet shall sound, and the dead shall be raised incorruptible, and we shall be changed."

Just wait until the day that the dead in Christ shall rise. Just wait until Jesus himself shall descend with a shout, and with the trump, and the voice of the archangel. Just wait until we all see that house not made with hands but made to last eternally by our Father in Heaven.

I say, "Just wait, just wait."

1

YOU MUST BE BORN AGAIN

"Thou art the Christ, the Son of the living God."
MATTHEW 16:16

"Verily, verily, I say unto thee, Except a man be born again, he cannot see the kingdom of God."
JOHN 3:3

If I could say just two things to you, I'd testify that Jesus is the Christ, the Son of the living God, and then tell you, "Truthfully, truthfully . . . you must be born again." You have to be born twice.

I was born the first time, and though I don't recall it myself, Momma told me all about it. But then, I was born again eleven years later. This time I told Momma all about it. I thank God I have been born twice.

Besides salvation texts (like John 3:16, "For God so loved the world, that He gave His only begotten Son, that whosoever believeth in him should not perish but have everlasting life"; Mark 16:16, "He that believeth and is baptized shall be saved";

and Romans 10:9, "If thou shalt confess with thy mouth the Lord Jesus, and shalt believe in thine heart that God hath raised him from the dead, thou shalt be saved") I consider the text "Thou are the Christ, the Son of the living God" the closest text to my heart. If by some way I should have advance knowledge of my last sermon on earth, I would preach from two great texts: Matthew 16, where Peter announces his belief in Jesus as the Christ; and John 3, where Jesus says to Nicodemus, "Truthfully, truthfully, I say unto you, you must be born again."

A WORD ABOUT FINDING KNOWLEDGE

Now when Nicodemus approached Jesus and called Him Rabbi, he was not belittling Jesus. Nicodemus knew Jesus wasn't a graduate of a school for rabbis. Nor was he acknowledged by the rabbinical association as a rabbi. But Nicodemus recognized there are two ways of getting knowledge. One is by formal education. All of you who are able to get it that way, be sure you get it. But don't make the false assumption that's the only way to get knowledge and understanding.

Not only can you get knowledge from education, but you can get it from divine revelation. God can reveal it to you. It is that kind of knowledge that caused Nicodemus to call Jesus Rabbi.

The same is true for us today. God has been the soul of my understanding. I am not a theologian. But sometimes I preach to theologians. I am not a graduate of a seminary, but I teach in a seminary. I have never had instructions on how to pastor, but I instruct pastors. They call on me from all over the world to instruct, for I got it from revelation. God revealed it to me. And I've been bold enough to do what God showed me to do. Sometimes what God shows you to do is fearful and awesome, but if you have courage—and the Lord tells you to do it—do it. God will back you up.

So, get an education. Get it well. But also pray for heavenly revelation.

That's why I always seek out a Christian doctor. I want a doctor who will be sufficiently trained but yet will look up and say, "Now God I'm looking to You for guidance. It's Your human body, and I want Your permission to let me go in there. When I get in there, won't You guide me?"

A while back, I visited Oral Roberts University, and I was interested in seeing their medical center. First I asked about the academic standing of their center. They had some of the highest people in the nation when it came to academics. The faculty had studied in the great schools of the nation. Then I asked about their faith. They are training doctors who believe they don't know it all. They believe there is a dimension only God can reveal. Now those are good doctors.

THE REAL ISSUE

When Nicodemus approached Jesus and called Him Rabbi on the basis of revelation, he was telling Jesus, "I know You are a great teacher."

But Jesus replied, in so many words, "Let's get down to the real issue. Let's dispense with your salutations and compliments. I know what I'm going to tell you already, and the quicker I get to it, the better it will be: You must be born again."

This was confusing because Nicodemus was a Pharisee, a member of the Sanhedrin council, a distinguished Jewish citizen. Why would Jesus tell him, "You must be born again"? Now if Jesus had been talking to the woman at the well—the one with many husbands—we could understand His saying to her, "You must be born again." If Jesus had been talking to the tax collector, we could understand His saying, "You must be born again." If He had been talking to the hypocritical Pharisees, we could understand His saying, "You must be born again." But telling Nicodemus, "You must be born again," presents a paradox.

First, Nicodemus was a high-ranking Jew. Therefore we can assume he was religious in conception and birth. He was well-bred and well-reared. He had been through the finest religious ceremonies. But Jesus said to Nicodemus, born to a religious family, "You must be born again."

Now there are some who feel because of who their mother is or was, that they have some special dispensation for salvation. But I tell them, "You must be born again."

There are even some members of the church who will tell you, "My uncle bought that pew. My daddy helped build the foundation. My momma was a leader in the choir. My grandma was around from the beginning." I appreciate what your family did, and you should, too. But I still have to tell you who are leaning on your momma or papa: those family members didn't get enough grace to save you too. "You must be born again."

Perhaps like you, Nicodemus responded, "How then can this be?" In other words, "How can you be discussing new birth with me? Don't you realize I am one of Abraham's offspring?"

But Jesus said, in essence, "As a matter of fact, I know Abraham. Before Abraham was, I Am. It is on the basis of what I know about your background that I'm telling you that you must be born again."

Why? Because before Abraham, we all had another relative, his name was Adam. The Jews always go back to Abraham, but Abraham had a daddy way back there and his name was Adam. If you keep digging way back there, I don't care what color or nationality you are, you had a daddy named Adam and a momma named Eve. So Jesus said, "On the basis of Adam you must be born again." All of us have someone in our background who was a stalwart for Christ, but that means nothing when we are confronted with the fact that each of us must be born again.

Just like brother Nicodemus, our birth is not our salvation, for it is not a matter of family background. Everyone, for himself, has to be born again.

But not only did Nicodemus have a great family background, he had a great religious conviction and great religious habits. He looked good religiously. Good from a hereditary standpoint. Good from a community standpoint. He's not only a Jew, he's a ruler of the Jews. From his birth he kept all the commandments. He kept the law perfectly from an outward manner. He prayed many times a day.

He did not eat without washing his hands. He did not consume that which the Law had forbidden. He didn't do this, and he didn't do that, and it was hard for Nicodemus to understand. I can imagine Nicodemus thinking, *He ought to be preaching to skid row, or to the prostitutes. Why is He telling me this?* But in spite of all these things, Jesus said, "You must be born again."

This is true of us today. We are like that. Since Nicodemus there have been many promoted to high offices in the church because of their looks or demeanor or their manner of speech, but they were not born again.

Nicodemus was holier than most. He was stricter than the most strict. Yet Jesus looked him in the eye and said, "You must be born again."

At this point, as most of us would, Nicodemus became silly. He said, "Ah, I know what you mean, you mean I must re-enter my mother's womb and come out again." But Jesus said, "Nicodemus, we're not on the same frequency. You're on FM and I'm on AM. You're talking about flesh; and I'm talking about spirit. Flesh is flesh, you certainly cannot reenter your mother's womb. Now sit down, Nicodemus, and let me get you straight."

If the qualities he presented were sufficient, there would be no need for the blood of Calvary. The problem Jesus showed Nicodemus is that he was only one-third alive—he was two-thirds dead. Man is flesh, but he is also spirit and soul. We all are in the same position. We are Adam's offspring. We are flesh and blood, but flesh and blood cannot enter the kingdom of heaven. We also have a spirit on the inside, and a soul. There was a time when Adam was alive both physically and spiritually. But sin entered the world, and our spirits and souls died. Only God's Spirit can make our spirits and souls alive again. Only He can give us the ability to worship Him or communicate with Him.

Jesus explained this to Nicodemus. "Man is a creature into which both physical and spiritual food can go. Nicodemus, long before you were born Adam disobeyed. At that moment he died spiritually and began to die physically. Ever since that day man is two-thirds dead. You are born in sin. You are in sin and in death."

Men are not born saved, they are born sinners, but they can become Christians. They must be born again. The man on the inside cannot become alive except by God. Nobody can awaken the deadness of a sinner but God.

Jesus' message to Nicodemus is the message that I give to you, "You must be born again."

2

HOW TO REJOICE ALWAYS

Rejoice in the Lord alway: and again I say, Rejoice.
PHILIPPIANS 4:4

Rejoice means "be full of joy." It must have been an important instruction, for Paul repeated it. "Rejoice in the Lord alway: and again I say, Rejoice." A Christian must be ever mindful of the kind of image the Lord expects us, as believers, to reflect: Be happy, be glad.

I might have written it, "Rejoice most of the time." If I could rewrite it that way, I suppose many of us could agree with it readily, because most of the time it's not too difficult to rejoice. Could you go along with that?

As I look back over my life I can certainly find moments of great rejoicing. I rejoiced when my pig won the grand championship. On days when apples and oranges would come to our little log cabin, I would rejoice. (I wasn't brought up in a community where you could go to the corner store and pick up apples and oranges.)

All through life I could rattle off high points. I remember when I got a telegram that said, You've been called to a church in Austin, Texas. I was nineteen years old and called to be pastor of a church. It was a great moment—certainly a time to rejoice.

JOY IN THE DOWN TIMES

But I can't truthfully say I haven't had some difficulty with this text that says "rejoice always." Because between the high mountain peaks there have been dark, dreary valleys. Valleys of sadness. When I was eleven years old I woke up and found the cold frame of Poppa. I've stood by the graves of countless loved ones. So I know something about the valleys that connect the mountains.

I know about reaching for something I thought was within my reach and yet missing it. I've calculated things only to find my figures were wrong. I know what it is to walk away with a downcast head. I know what it is to be informed that it was my best friend who plunged the dagger into my heart, that the one I considered my best supporter was really against me.

When I consider these experiences, I have trouble in the admonition to rejoice always. I would have no trouble saying "sometimes," but always?

So let us try to see here: Is there a program? Whenever the Lord tells us to do something, He gives us a program. If we follow it, He will lead us to His goal for us. Most of God's commandments begin with His first statement, in this case to rejoice always. Then we have to follow up with various references and contexts.

In this text, the apostle Paul says, "Rejoice." He means there is no reason for Christians to be in the dark, to be disgusted, to be in depression or despair. Yet, if we really try to rejoice *always,* even in times when it doesn't seem reasonable, people may think we are crazy. I had a professor when I was in college who was known as the number one nut on the campus. Everybody said, "He's crazy." Why? Every time somebody met up with him he'd tip his hat and say, "Good morning, sir, good morning, ma'am." Even today if you're not frowning and fuming, people may say you're not ordinary.

Ours should not be the mindset of a bitter quarrelsome person. We need to be radiant, beautiful, full of joy and rejoicing. It need not be an overblown enthusiastic Hollywood production. All we need is to be plain and simple, rejoicing. When you see me laughing and talking, it doesn't mean that I haven't had a storm; it just means I have a storm stopper.

MAKING IT PRACTICAL

How shall we accomplish this? Let's go to Philippians 4:13, "I can do all things through Christ which strengtheneth me." To accomplish these things we must do it *through Christ.* If we don't have a right relationship, if we have not accepted Christ, if we don't have Jesus in proper focus, if He is not an indwelling personality in us, we can't do it.

The world's too mean to be happy every day, that is, if you don't have an inside source. You'll suffer disappointment if you don't have inner peace. You'll have too many inner storms if you don't have that inner peace. You need to have someone who can say, "Peace, be still."

I've been through the storms. But I have somebody who can say, "Peace, be still." But to have this you've got to start with Jesus. You might say it doesn't matter who you start with, just so you start. Well, that's not so.

Now take Buddha; he can't calm your storm. He's just a statue with hands that can't heal, feet that can't walk, a mouth that can't talk, and eyes that can't see. You can't chant enough to get the storms of life to subside for you. You've got to have the storm stopper Jesus to succeed in calming the storm.

The only answer is in the man who calmed the waters. Time and space don't allow me to tell you all the things I have done that I didn't know I could do. I didn't know I could get to the point where I could bless my enemies. But I had to start with Jesus.

Once you know Jesus you begin to know the inner secrets of life. As Philippians 4:12 says, "I know both how to be abased, and I know how to abound." Most of us are prepared to abound. I have a sermon I preach that says most of us are prepared for God's blessing, but we can't rejoice when He starts saying no.

I know what it is to abound, but I also know what it's like to be down and out. I know what it is to lose. You probably do, too. Some of us have lost what we wanted most, while wanting to abound in everything. That's why there are so many casualties among preachers who tell people that whatever they want all they have to do is believe and claim it to receive it. That's just not so. Let me tell you the truth: There are a whole lot of things you reach for that you're not gonna get.

There are preachers who say, "You never have to be sick, you can just claim it." Let me tell you the truth: I don't care what you say, you can claim it all you want, but it's probably not gonna happen.

BEING JOYFUL WHEN GOD SAYS NO

There's nowhere in the Book where you show me a person who claimed everything and got everything. God withholds.

When God says no that's as much an answer to prayer as yes.

Someone might say, "I prayed, and God didn't hear me." Yes He did. He hears the faintest whisper. He heard your prayers, but in His divine wisdom and for His own reasons He said no.

We are not accustomed, nor prepared, to have no for an answer. But the apostle says, you've got too much good in your life from God's hand to be downhearted. When I don't have it, I'm thanking God for what I'm about to receive. When it passes me by, I thank Him for having the wisdom to deny it. You've got to know how to abound and be denied. Verse 12 goes on to say, "I know both how to be abased, and I know how to abound: everywhere and in all things I am instructed both to be full and to be hungry, both [how] to abound and to suffer need." You cannot match your demand with what you deserve. You can't go around and say, "I demand it, because I deserve it." Whatever He gives you comes from His undeserved favor. His gifts are evidences of His favor; we could do nothing to merit them.

Because people do not know how to live rejoicing, they find nothing to rejoice about in ordinary living. They come into my office and ask, What do I have to be rejoicing about? I always answer: Number one, you are living. Number two, you had enough health to come in here. Number three, when you looked in the mirror you knew who you were. Number four, you have some children. Number five, you live in a country that helps you with your children when you can't find where their daddies are. Now shout over that, because if you were in another country they might just take the children and sterilize you.

When we don't know how to rejoice at ordinary things, we miss the opportunity to rejoice altogether.

I rejoiced when I had eight suits and had to ponder over which suit to wear. There was a time when I only had one suit, and it's an improvement when I have to decide which suit I'm going to wear. But I was and am happy in both situations. I know how to do without, and I know about plenty.

I know how it is to preach in the White House; I've preached there. But then, I know how to have a good time in a storefront. I've met and counseled with five presidents of the United States. But I enjoy preaching to two or three people who live daily, more ordinary lives.

I know how to abound and be abased. I know how to be filled and to be hungry. I know how to suffer need. But the key to success in either state is knowing Jesus. This is a tough world, and (I've said this before and I'll say it again) if you can't take it, you can't make it. And if you can't make it, there's not too many people who will care.

You have to toughen up. Our whole society has to toughen up. The apostle Paul could rejoice even in a jail while many of us can live in luxury houses and can't rejoice. Check verse 11, "Not that I speak in respect of want: for I have learned," [see— it's a learning process] "in whatsoever state I am, therewith to be content." I've learned that no matter my state, God has something for me to do. If I'm in the jailhouse, I still have my pride, I look and see why God has relegated me to the jailhouse. You can't make me cry, for whatever state I'm in, I know how to rejoice.

DON'T JUST HEAR IT—DO IT

In verse 9 we read, "Those things, which ye have both learned, and received, and heard, and seen in me, do: and the God of peace shall be with you."

You cannot have peace simply because you've heard a whole lot; the devils have heard, sinners have heard, but you've got to get around to doing what you've heard—learning and receiving it. That's when the joy comes. Joy is hooked up with doing. If you won't do what God says, you won't have joy. You cannot have rest or be perfectly blessed until you've become a doer of His Word, instead of just a hearer.

Get up every morning, get your Bible in your hand, get on your knees and walk with God, talk with God. Worship the Lord. Become doers of the Word and not hearers only. The more you do, the more you will rejoice.

Some of you are sad because you've not done anything God has asked you to do. At funerals there are a whole lot of families who cannot rejoice, because they've just been hearers and not doers. They've depended on momma or papa to be their salvation. The joy follows when you walk with God.

GOOD THOUGHTS

Let's glance back from verse 9 to verse 8. "Finally, brethren, whatsoever things are true, whatsoever things are honest, whatsoever things are just, whatsoever things are pure, whatsoever things are lovely, whatsoever things are of good report; if there be any virtue, and if there be any praise, think on these things."

In crass terms, we might say, "Get your mind out of the gutter." You can't rejoice because you've got too much guilt in your head. Got too many lies you've told. That's why it says to get your mind in order. You're thinking about too many things that aren't true, honest, or just. Your thinking has cut off your rejoicing. You've got to start thinking about truth, honesty, justice, purity, loveliness, things of good report. If you do that, true rejoicing will be your reward.

You've got to stop thinking about soap operas and movie mysteries and the nightly news. Get your mind off those things and think of *these* things. You start with Jesus being your example, you clean up your mind, and whatever is still

bugging you, tell God about it. Then what do you do? Back in
verses 6 and 7, Paul writes, "Be careful for nothing; but in every
thing by prayer and supplication with thanksgiving let your requests be made known unto God. And the peace of God, which
passeth all understanding, shall keep your hearts and minds
through Christ Jesus."

This is the clincher. This is our reason to rejoice. You've
done your homework. You've got your mind on the things that
are clean and pure. Now you're ready for God to do something.
It says, "And the peace of God, which passeth all understanding, shall keep your hearts and minds." Now that's something
to rejoice about. He doesn't offer that peace for only the good
situations. Read it again, it doesn't qualify where or when, it
just promises the peace of God will keep itself fresh and new in
your heart and in your mind.

Rejoice, I say, rejoice. In a jailhouse, rejoice; if all the world
has turned against you, rejoice. This one thing I know, whatever your circumstance the Lord will be with you.

Rejoice, and again I say, rejoice.

HOW TO ESCAPE DEPRESSION

*"Come unto me all ye that labour and are heavy laden,
and I will give you rest."*

MATTHEW 11:28

According to a survey taken recently, 69 percent of the population of the United States possess a negative attitude. That means that sixty-nine out of every 100 people have a negative and broken spirit. When a person says good morning to them, they reply, "What's good about it?"

There are two ways a person generally expresses himself first thing in the morning. One is: "My lord, another day." The other is: "Thank you, Lord, for another day." While one says, "It's no use trying; I know I ain't gonna make it," the other says, "I know I'll make it if I try."

Let me give you another example. A shoe salesman went to Africa and wired back, "Send my return ticket. There's no use trying; nobody wears shoes here." Another shoe salesman in the same position wired his office with this message: "Send enough money to open a factory; everybody needs shoes here."

Every time I preach to a congregation of a thousand people, 690 of them carry a negative and broken spirit. This negative spirit impairs their will to cope with this competitive world. If they possess nothing but gripes, the world consigns them to the slow lane. Eventually they'll get the message: "Why don't you just stop trying altogether?"

When I go home at night, there are times when my wife talks about problems. But not every night. I don't come home to talk about the problems we have. That's not even the best way to solve them.

NEGATIVE SINNERS AND POSITIVE SAINTS

Now this is all understandable for those who are sinners, outside the world where Christ is Lord. After all, a sinner does not have in him that which causes him to be positive. If he is surrounded with negativism, he'll project negativism. According to the apostle Paul, the sinner has no life, no God, no salvation, no hope. That's why the Scriptures tell us not to be unequally yoked with an unsaved person. When you are confronted by a negative person, that negativity can begin to reach you in your own spirit. When you marry someone who is full of spiritual negativism, he or she will always try to prove you are wrong and won't accept that you could be right.

Now, on the other hand, because I know God, I have something to be positive about. He makes me keep on keepin' on, when all around me seems hopeless.

How is it that people who have hope may initially get depressed but soon rise above it? How is it that the people who have in them the same power that raised Jesus from the dead are able to cope? Well, the key is that very power. There's no greater problem than being raised from the dead. Is your problem greater than that? God demonstrated that He had all power because He conquered both death and the grave. Then He says, "That same power which enabled me to rise again and walk away from the grave is in you." How can you keep wallowing in negativism? Because this same power dwells in you, you can overcome your circumstance—no matter what it is.

THE SOURCE OF NEGATIVISM

That said, though, we need to discuss this matter of how we got into such a state of depression, before we discuss the way to escape it. I'm not talking about clinical depression caused by chemical imbalance—a physical problem in the brain. I am talking about the negative feelings that can overtake us if we don't use God's principles to control them.

First, we become depressed because we become overwhelmed. Whether you are a saint or a sinner you can become overwhelmed with life's situations. You can become overwhelmed just by going to your mailbox and picking up mail that bears a negative message. You can be like the man who said, "Every company in town is after me—light bill, gas bill, telephone." You can just pick up your mail and become overwhelmed. I can testify to that. I often get to the mail before my wife has a chance to launder it. It's depressing. Yes, my friend, it's really depressing.

You can wake up in the morning and look to your right, look to your left, and look in front and behind you, and there are so many unanswered situations. Though those are the same problems you faced when you went to sleep; even a night of rest has not erased them. They're still with you.

Friends can overwhelm you. If you're available, that

telephone can bring enough bad news into your house to over-whelm you. As pastor of my church I receive as many as a hundred telephone calls every day. Ninety-nine percent of them are problems. They wouldn't call the pastor if there were not problems. Which means that I deal with that many problems every day.

If you have compassion and the love of God in you, you share a part of you with everybody you talk to. So it stands to reason that when you give of yourself ninety times a day, it does become overwhelming. You are tempted to go somewhere and say, "Sorry, I'm not in."

I don't care how tough you are, I don't care how many degrees you have, I don't care how much knowledge you have—life can overwhelm you. You can be hit from so many different directions that you can get the crazy idea, "I'm just gonna end it all." But there's another part of just ending it all: Don't forget you've got to face it all in eternity.

There's some kind of false heresy going around that, when I'm dead I'm done. The fact remains that you cannot give life nor can you terminate life of your own will. For as soon as you have stopped breathing in this world, you'll awaken in eternity. There you'll be called to stand and explain why you couldn't trust Him. Remember, our Savior promised never to leave us alone.

The opposite of this is that you can become overwhelmed by circumstances but enjoy the protection of God's army. You remember the story of the prophet in 2 Kings 6? A young man awoke and saw the city surrounded with enemies. He didn't see any way out. That's how our lives can be sometimes. You can be surrounded with enemies. It doesn't have to be people, it can be circumstances, unsolved problems, unmet needs, all sorts of things.

You remember when the prophet awoke and saw what the young man saw. He went to his closet and got on his knees and said, "Lord, I pray thee, open his eyes that he may see. And the Lord opened the eyes of the young man; and he saw: and, behold, the mountain was full of horses and chariots of fire round about Elisha"(verse 17). He is seeing enemies, and the enemies have surrounded the city. But God lets him see that the enemies are surrounded by horses and chariots of fire that He has provided. If you can't see beyond the first level you will enter deep depression about the worthlessness of living. When you see little progress and it seems all is against you, that's when you can enter into depression.

Another way to fall to depression's grip is when you see the prosperity of the wicked. Yes, how well wicked folks prosper can cause Christian folks to become depressed.

Here you try to do right, here you try to be moral, try to live by what pastor preaches, and still it looks like you're overwhelmed every day, while you see someone who does not try to live to honor God, who does not have reverence for God, who does not try to obey His commandments—and that person does nothing but prosper. Here you drive an old Ford and he drives a new Mercedes Benz. Now, that can depress you.

If I were God, I'd let the man who walks with God drive the new car. But I'm not God. I wouldn't let people use me as even I have used God. I wouldn't let people sit in church on Sunday and make vows and pledges, yet during the week break those vows and live like the rest of the world. And then on the Lord's day, instead of being in the house of prayer they talk about their yacht and about shacking up somewhere down in Mexico or out in Las Vegas, then on Monday morning they say, "Lord, bless me on the job." I'd say, "Where have you been since you spoke to me?" That's what I'd say if I were God.

I can't explain it. He blesses men who don't even think about Him. He blesses people who never even say, "Thank you, Lord." Yet there are those who are trying to walk uprightly, to raise their children right, and it looks like it's just one crisis after another. The prophet Jeremiah (Jeremiah 12:1) says the prosperity of the wicked almost got him; often we're tempted to say the same. The psalmist has a similar reaction when he looks around at the prosperity of the wicked (Psalm 73:3-12). They walk around arrogantly with stiff necks, they neither bow their hearts or minds to God.

Yet I walk uprightly, and I try to follow God's command, and it looks like good things always pass me by. Of course that can send you into a depression. All I can say is you've got to keep on doing what you are doing, no matter what people say or what the circumstances are.

BREAKING DEPRESSION'S GRIP

Now I've spoken about how you can get into depression, give me a little space to tell you how you can get out.

If you are a Christian and you are depressed, the first thing I advise is: Reread the contract. I said, reread the contract. You may be depressed over what God has never promised. He never promised that you could keep up with the Joneses. He never promised you a brown mink coat on Monday, a black mink on Tuesday, a white one on Wednesday, and a gray one on Sunday.

Most Christians do not refer to the contract. Rather, they refer to their imagination as to what Christianity ought to be like. I heard a preacher on the radio say, "If my father was rich and didn't give me food to eat, no place to sleep, I wouldn't serve a God like that." Well, he hasn't read the contract.

Not only may you not have a place to sleep, His own Son

had no place to lay His head. Not only may it get rough on you, but it got tougher on Jesus. They did not crown Him as Lord, they did not give Him houses and lands, silver and gold. They did not honor Him, or dress Him in royal robes as the Son of God.

Read the contract. They raised Him high, they dropped Him low, they riveted His hands and feet, they spit on Him, they put thorns on His head, they pierced His side, they gambled over His clothes. The Bible says, if they did that to the Son of God, His followers ought to expect the same (John 15:18).

If you read this contract you will discover we are caught up in warfare. We don't wrestle against flesh and blood opponents but against principalities and powers of darkness, spiritual wickedness in high places (Ephesians. 6:12). The contract says some of us will be put in prison and, for the sake of His Name, may suffer loss (Hebrews 11:36-38).

Now when you get depressed, understand what spirit is trying to depress you. It's surely not God's Spirit. For example, the apostle Paul in the bottom of the ship is not depressed; in jail, not depressed. In fact he wrote in a letter from jail: "I count it an honor to be counted worthy to suffer for the name of the Lord." He understood the contract.

This world knows nothing of grace, but we are children of grace. This world is no friend to grace. This world is no friend to God's family. This world is no friend to God's children. We are pilgrims.

This world ain't my home, I'm just a pilgrim passing through this barren land. Please listen to me, don't reject these words: You must observe this contract. Though you have been mutilated by friends, expect it—it's in the contract. If your name has been scandalized for Him, it's in the contract. If you weren't saved, the devil wouldn't take you to task, but because you are God's child you must endure what the contract calls for. This contract says that even though I walk through the valley of the shadow of death I will fear no evil.

A PROMISE TO LIVE BY

Thank God, though, that's not all. There's something else in this contract. He said, "Lo, I am with you alway" (Matthew 28:20). That's my picker-upper, that's my high, and though I may be in the valley, or on the mountaintop, if Jesus goes with me I'll go anywhere.

It is not mine to question the judgments of my Lord, it is but mine to follow the leading of His Word. But if to go or stay, or whether here or there, I'll be with my Savior, content anywhere.

Thank God if it's in the lion's den, there's no depression. If it's in the fiery furnace, there's no depression. Even if it's on a hill called Calvary, there's no depression. If I have possessions, I'm fine, or if I have nothing, I'm fine. I'm satisfied with Jesus alone.

Thank God this is the pathway out of depression if we will remember that Jesus has promised never, never to leave us alone. Never alone. If you keep His promises He will supply all your needs—maybe not all your wants, but all your needs. He has promised that He will fight your battles. He has promised He will make your enemies your footstool. He has promised joy as your portion. He has promised patience for your trials. He may not move the mountain, but He will give you strength to cross it. Read His contract.

Remember, when you suffer depression, it is just temporary, for God's Word promises, "Joy cometh in the morning" (Psalm 30:5). As John Newton wrote in his beloved hymn,

"Amazing Grace," I've been through "many dangers, toils and snares" but God's "grace has brought me safe thus far and grace will lead me home."

Read the contract, trust God's Word. I'll say it again, read the contract.

4

WHY THE STRUGGLE?

*"But he knoweth the way that I take: when he hath tried me,
I shall come forth as gold."*

JOB 23:10

The honest confession of every one of us would be that, though we are born again, sanctified, and filled with the Holy Ghost—life is still a struggle. If you're not presently in one kind of a struggle or the other, save up that strength, because a struggle is right around the corner.

Today, believers are having financial difficulties. Genuine, praying, tithing believers are having difficulties making ends meet. God-fearing parents are having trouble with children. Honest Christians are being lied to and talked about without cause. The Christian life is a struggle.

I see no description in Scripture of a Christian journey in which there is no warfare. I'm unable to find in Scripture a

calm, cross-less life. All the lives that have been crowned with
the benediction of God are lives that have known what it means
to struggle. I have not known a period in my own life when I
have not had troubles and trials.

I was born in the middle of the Great Depression—a struggle.
The year after I was born my father left my mother—another
struggle. Two years later my mother bundled up four children
and went begging for a job. When I was four years old, a kind
lady asked my mother to let her raise me in her two-room log
cabin in the country. There I lived with her and her husband
(whom I called Poppa), eating peanuts, hickory nuts, hoecakes,
molasses, and fat meat. At eleven years old I woke up to find
Poppa dead in his chair.

And there in the two-room log cabin with no aid to depen-
dent children, with no welfare, and Momma too young to get
old-age assistance, we lived off of the goodwill of people who
lived nearby. Neil Walker gave us a gallon of milk. Mr. Cary gave
us a few sweet potatoes. Dick Salmers gave us a slice of bacon.

I graduated from a four-teacher, twelve-grade school that had
no heating system other than logs in an old furnace. I had to crawl
out of the log cabin and have four fires blazing by eight o'clock
after having milked five cows for Hick Somers for $1.25 a week.

And so I don't know life without struggles.

We live in an age where we must understand that the Scriptures affirm that born-again people will have struggles. Jesus
said, in John 16:33, "In the world ye shall have tribulation."
Elsewhere we read, in Psalm 34:19, "Many are the afflictions
of the righteous."

SISTER HARRISON'S RESPONSE TO STRUGGLE

Some of God's choice Christians have been on that bed of
affliction year in and year out.

On Thanksgiving morning several years ago, I went to visit Sister Harrison. I walked into her room and saw the most beautiful smile coming from anybody that I've ever seen. She reached over to me and said, "Ain't God good?" And I had to stand there and tremble, wondering what Sister Harrison had that made her smile. You see, Sister Harrison had no eyes and no legs. Both eyes out and both legs cut off, and yet in the middle of her bed she says, "God is good." Then she knocked me to my knees when she continued, "I wonder what I've done so good that the Lord would let my pastor come and see me." She said, "I'm unworthy, I'm unworthy of the pastor taking off from his busy schedule to come and see me."

And I just said, "Oh Lord, forgive me." It floored me to think she would consider it an honor for me to come, when in fact I am humbled by her presence. I preach about what she knows about. It's a struggle. It's a struggle. But God is still good.

Crime is on the increase, because some young man has looked at life and decided, "I'm not going to struggle. I'm going to take this sister's life, and I'm going to rob a bank because I've been poor long enough. I'm not going to struggle."

The desire of modern-day Christians is to get rid of the struggle. Let me be happy, let me be prosperous. Let me be full of joy. Let me enjoy life. Give me a split-level home, give me an air conditioned house, give me two cars. But not the struggle. Not the struggle. I'm not made for struggle.

There are those who have gone from smoking to marijuana to avoid the struggle. There are those who have hated the struggle so much that they have gone to cocaine. They want to get high. They know they have to come down. But if just for a few days they can get up there where there's no struggle and forget the problems and forget the bills and forget the worries, they're willing to take a chance.

A STRUGGLE-FREE CHURCH

I'm going to come on down now to the fact that in answer to the quest of those who don't want to struggle, we have built struggle-free churches. We listen to preachers who say you don't have to struggle. I've seen preachers build great congregations on the gospel of the greenback. Their message is, "What are you doing broke, honey? Building gold is the law. Cattle on a thousand hills belong to the Lord. And you say you don't have any money? You're in the wrong church. You've got to come and join our church, where everybody's prosperous."

I was in Chicago, and one preacher said he didn't even want more members with problems to come to his church. Why? Because, "We have a God that has everything and there's something wrong with your faith if you are God's child and God owns everything, and you ain't got nothing," he said. He was saying, if you're struggling, there's something wrong with your faith. If that is true, then gamblers who have never been in church ought to become deacons. If the greenbacks are the judgment stick for salvation then Onassis should have been the pope. And if dollar bills are the yardstick of faith, then Christ was a flunky. If a bank account is the measure of faith then my momma had none. We could look up through the ceiling of our log cabin and see the stars. We could look down through the floors and see air. But it was a house of faith.

WHERE DOES THE STRUGGLE COME FROM?

Why is it a struggle? Well, first of all it's a struggle because the fruits of our sin must be manifested in this world. We're all descendants of one who had the malady of sin in his veins. We are descendants of Adam. And Adam did not have a slight stumble. Nor a small casualty. He had a fatal fall. Sin entered the bloodstream of Adam and therefore it entered the entire world and everything in it. There are those who claim that man did not fall. The humanists suggest all men are born good, not bad. But the cold facts are: we are born in sin. You don't have to teach a child anything bad. Just let him get older. He'll act sinfully. We have the sin in our bloodstream. I have in my body genes from a daddy, mannerisms of my great-grandfather, but the most obvious traits that I have go back not to my daddy, not to my grandfather, but to Adam. It's the stuff that Adam left in me that makes me do wrong, even when I want to do good.

Evil is all around. It's the stuff that Adam left in me that makes me break every command God ever gave me. My stiff-neckedness. My disobedience. My quickness to sin. My hot temper. My unwillingness to obey God. And though sin was forgiven on the cross—and it was forgiven—the truth of sin as manifested in the condemned must manifest itself in this world.

My forgiveness gives me a perfect position, but I still have a terminal condition. My position is, I'm saved. But my condition is I'm struggling. I'm trying. "There is therefore now no condemnation in [me] because I am in Christ Jesus." But in my flesh there's a war going on. In Adam it's a struggle. Our hair comes out. Our teeth fall out. Our eyes grow dim. Our steps get short. We are fallen, we are stumbling, we are down, we are struggling, we are dying because we are offspring of a fallen race.

Scripture is clear on this point:

For all have sinned, and come short of the glory of God.
—ROMANS 3:23

All we like sheep have gone astray.
—ISAIAH 53:6

I have sinned. I'm not proud of it. I'm fallen. I wish it weren't so. But since I've been conquered by sin, I have willfully and deliberately and knowingly done wrong in the sight of God. The payoff of sin is a struggle. Sin will catch up with you. Sin will bring you down. Sin will shut your mouth. Sin will dry your spirit. Sin will cut your "shout" off.

When I didn't know any better, I thought I was pretty good. But when I made a study of the "thou shall nots" and all the other sins of omission and commission listed in the Book, I said, "Woe is me! For I am undone; because I am a man of unclean lips" (Isaiah 6:5). The good news is, though, that although I'm unworthy to even touch this Book, the Lord has called me to preach the gospel. The Lord said to me, "I did not call you in the light of your righteousness, but I called you in spite of your sins."

PAINFUL PROCESS OF PERFECTING

But there is yet another struggle that will not quit for believers. We who are born-again Christians are undergoing a process—we are being saved, being sanctified, being perfected. That process is a painful process. We are filthy rags being washed in the blood of the Lamb. We are crooked sticks being straightened out by the anvil of the gospel. We are dirty folk being cleaned up. The process is called sanctification; it starts at regeneration, and it goes through to glorification.

Glorification doesn't happen down here. Because we have to get rid of this old house. Before you can be glorified you must have another body not made with hands. A sinner is a lump of clay on the shelf with nobody doing anything to it. A sinner is a lump of clay that nobody bought. But a Christian is a lump of clay off the shelf and in the hands of the Master. The Master takes that clay and arranges it, twists it, molds it, rolls it, pounds it, breaks it up, and puts it in the fire. What does that sound like, my friend? Struggles, struggles, struggles, struggles. It hurts me, this refining process. But that's all right, because we become more than a lump of clay in the Master's hands.

In the book of Job we read of a righteous man's struggles. His friends kept saying to him, "Job, you're struggling, Job, you're having a hard time. Job, what's wrong with you?"

Job said to them, "I don't know. What's wrong with me? I lost my children. I lost my wealth. I lost everything I had, but I know there's something going on here. For He knows my heart. He knows I've done nothing wrong. He knows I've tried and tried and tried. And in all of the trying I'm still struggling."

Job said, "Here it is. I'm under inspection. I'm under construction. I don't look good because He's still working on me. I don't look good because He's still building on me. I don't look good because He's not through, but after a while when He's through with me I'll shine like never before. So, don't be so hard on me. He's not through with me—yet."

5

THE EXPERIENCE OF A DRY BROOK

Elijah was a man with a nature like ours, and he prayed earnestly that it would not rain; and it did not rain on the land for three years and six months. And he prayed again, and the heaven gave rain, and the earth produced its fruit.

JAMES 5:17–18 (NKJV)

One of the most exciting times to be a Christian is on one of those rare days when God is acting like we think God ought to act.

The assumption on the part of man is that he knows enough to instruct God. I've heard people say, "Well, pastor, I prayed. I told God, and He didn't do it. I don't know what's wrong with God." The terrible assumption is that we believe our prayers are perfect plans; if we could just get God to do what we tell Him, the way we tell Him, everything would be perfect. What we don't understand is that God doesn't see it the way we see it.

And yet there are a few happy days in our lives when God is

doing exactly what we think He should do. Then there are the other kind of days.

Elijah, in this text, experiences both of those kinds of days. Let's drop in on Elijah when he is at his height of joy in 1 Kings 17:1-6, when God is acting exactly the way we (and His prophet) think He should act:

> *And Elijah the Tishbite, who was of the inhabitants of Gilead, said unto Ahab, As the LORD God of Israel liveth, before whom I stand, there shall not be dew nor rain these years, but according to my word. And the word of the LORD came unto him, saying, Get thee hence, and turn thee eastward, and hide thyself by the brook Cherith, that is before Jordan. And it shall be, that thou shalt drink of the brook; and I have commanded the ravens to feed thee there. So he went and did according unto the word of the LORD: for he went and dwelt by the brook Cherith, that is before Jordan. And the ravens brought him bread and flesh in the morning, and he drank of the brook.*

The Lord has just told Elijah it's not going to rain for three years—until the Lord says rain. It must have been an exciting time for the prophet Elijah, who was to deliver this news. God's talking to him to give him a special message to give to the people. The prophet always gets a lot of joy out of hearing from God, but he gets even more joy when God has decided to decree judgment against the wickedness of men. And Elijah has already been vexed over what Ahab has permitted to go on at the behest of Jezebel, his wife. So Elijah is rejoicing in receiving word that the Lord is going to do something about Jezebel just prancing around unbridled. The judgment is that there isn't going to be any rain. Now, there's a lot of suffering in this, but a man of God would prefer seeing the folks suffer than for them to continue defying the word of the Lord.

And so Elijah tells the king and the people, "It's not going to rain for three years."

But then God says to Elijah, "Now as far as you are concerned, you get up now and go eastward; I've got a brook that's flowing. There you'll drink."

Now, you know that excited him. A special brook of cool and flowing water, protected from this drought. And then God informs Elijah a raven will bring the prophet fresh bread and fresh meat in the morning and the evening. So, God tells him, "And all I am asking you to do is sleep by the brook, get up and eat and drink some water and go to sleep again." Now, this is a great moment. Being personally taken care of by God. Isn't that something? God instructing him to go where there is water. God is acting toward His prophet exactly as God should act.

BE CAREFUL, LEST YOU FALL

Put yourself in Elijah's situation, in our day and age. What if something happened in Los Angeles—or in the city where you live—and there was no water and no food, but in the midnight hour God came to you and told you where to go to find fresh water. And that in the morning a raven—a falcon-type bird—would come and deliver fresh, piping hot bread with well-roasted meat. You'd feel mighty exalted. You would have a moment of ecstasy. Because that's the way God ought to take care of His faithful prophet.

Here this prophet is, standing up against the king. Here this prophet is, standing up against the false prophets. Here this prophet is, standing up against the hostility of the nation that has rebelled against God. Here this preacher has proclaimed the gospel and people have gotten mad at him and won't cooperate and have sat down on him and won't give him a love offering.

Yet God prepares him a menu and fresh water—that preacher would feel all right, wouldn't he? He would feel vindicated. He would feel that God has not left him alone.

In not too many verses Elijah is about to experience a terrible feeling when the devil suggests that he is all alone. But for now, the raven is on time. The dinner is beautiful. The water is fresh. And Elijah is happy.

So it is in your life and my life. We can remember when, in a sense, God has sent His raven and sent His blessings. And they have been right on time. We've sat down and calculated life; we've said our prayers and paid our tithes, sung in the choir, gone out witnessing. Life just floats by on time. We have a joy that God is blessing us right now. That's a great feeling.

That's also a great moment for the devil to hit you a hard lick—when God is acting like God ought to act. When God is sending the blessings. When we are out of a job, He sends us another one before the first one is over. When money is low, something happens and we find more money. When we get sick, we pray and God delivers us. When we get in trouble we pray and it clears up. That's God acting like He ought to act.

But then, if you keep reading it says the brook dried up and the raven tarried. Now, the dry brook was not something new, because all of those in the area were being affected by the drought. There were other dry brooks. Everybody had dry brooks. Nobody could find any wheat to cook fresh bread. Nobody could find any trickling brooks, so that wasn't anything new. But it was new in the experience of this prophet. It was new for him. And so it is for us as Christians. One day we are faced with things that other folks are facing every day. Sometimes we are God's spoiled children. God has done so well in taking care of us, God has been so good to us so long, until we experience what others have experienced every day and what many have experienced throughout life—then God isn't acting like we think He ought to act. Something must be wrong with God.

GOD'S GENEROUS PROVISION; OUR RESPONSIBILITIES

We who are here today, if we would come up against one moment where we didn't have food to eat, that would be shocking to us. A young man called me on the telephone and he said, "My child doesn't have any food, and we haven't had any food. And I want to know what you're going to do about it. You are a pastor of a church." And the first thing I had to do was pray. That's the first thing I had to do. Because you have to pray before you answer folks like that, so you won't injure them, or spoil them. The first thing I wanted to say was that it wasn't my child. In this country we need to tell some of these fellows, "That isn't my child." Don't walk up here with your children as if these children are not yours. It's your child, first of all. The first responsibility of what we're going to do about that hungry child ought to be mama and papa's. If you know you have a check that's supposed to last thirty days, don't spend it in fifteen. And if you can't keep up with the Joneses, settle down with the Smiths.

A woman walked into my office and said, "You don't know anything about poverty, driving your Lincoln and sleeping in your house." That's where I am now, honey. And that's where you could have been had you saved some.

I can speak authoritatively, because ain't nobody in town has been as poor as I have been. Nobody in here has known poverty like I have known it. I had peanuts for breakfast and watermelon for dinner. I know about poverty. But Momma, somehow or other, got godly wisdom where molasses and fat meat and hoecakes lasted us. I'm glad God brought me up like He did. Because some of you could fool me had I not come up the way I did.

LESSONS IN THE LEAN TIMES

When you wake up to a dry brook, don't think that something went wrong with God. When God doesn't act the way we think He should, we get upset with Him. But then we discover that there are other folk who have been getting along on what you have been throwing away. There are children right now who didn't get anything for breakfast. They are now dying in the arms of some Somali or some Haitian woman. Their brooks have been dried all along.

God's all right. You don't have to check Him. There is nothing wrong with Him, and He has heard your prayer. He has just decided to give you the experience of a dry brook.

Dry brooks can teach you something. Tarrying ravens can teach you something. When that contract, when that check, when that order just keeps flying around but won't come down, it can teach you something. You don't have to check out God or His health, or His hearing capacity. You just have to adjust to living by a dry brook. That's what you have to do.

But when the raven tarried and the brook dried, notice if you please that Elijah didn't panic. He stayed on the job. There is nowhere in the record where he charged God foolishly. He never got up and said, "I'm here because You sent me here, and now the brook where You sent me is dry." He just waited at his duty post. And that's what you've got to do. Trials of this world cannot knock you out when you are tarrying for God. Just stay on the battlefield.

> *Trials dark on every hand, we cannot understand,*
> *All the ways that God would lead us to the blessed*
> *promised land.*

Just stay on the job. Dry brooks must not let you fall out

with God. Contracts that you did not get must not let you fall out with God. Promotions that you thought you deserved must not let you fall out with God.

They that wait on the Lord will hear another instruction. Some of you get up and run with no instructions, get up and run when trouble comes, but I say to you: just wait there until the same voice that told you to come here tells you where else to go. Wait there. Wait there.

And incidentally, the brook dried while Elijah was doing the will of the Lord. Now, that's a rough one. You see, if you're living in sin, if you're living contrary to the will of God and the brook dries up, you can say, "Lord, I'm guilty. I know exactly why the brook dried up." But when the brook dries up while you're doing what God told you to do, that's a jolt. But stay at the brook. The same voice that came to you will come to you once again. And He'll give you more instructions.

A Fresh Supply

Then the Lord said to Elijah, "Get up and go over to a widow's house and tell her to fix you dinner. I'm switching now from raven to widow. And tell her to fix you something to eat. When you get over there she will only have just a little. And it's just enough for her child and her, and they plan on dying. But I'm going to connect your needs with her needs, and I'm going to bless both of you. Now, she's going to have to stand the test, too, because you must instruct her to fix you a cake out of her last meal." She has to stand the test, too. Everybody has to stand God's test.

Elijah went in there, and she was knocking out the meal barrel. He said, "I'm a preacher; fix me some dinner."

She said, "But I only have enough for a last meal for myself."

"Fix it for me."

And this woman didn't say, "Do you understand that this is my last?" Instead she said, "Sit down and rest yourself; it will be done in nothing flat."

I could almost hear the whimpering of the child when he saw that last cake going off the table, on into the room for the preacher. "Momma, was that all?"

"Yes."

"And we're giving it to the preacher?"

"Yes."

"Why?"

Now, you all don't believe it, but the old folk believed it. Old folk believed if that's the last, give it to God's man. It's no secret how we made it. We had godly faith. And Elijah ate well. Pains and groans in these stomachs, standing there watching him. And then he said, "Sugar, go back to that empty bag, and you will not only find another meal, but you will find a meal and a meal and a meal and a meal. Because you have obeyed."

Hallelujah! Obey God. Stay there until you get His next word. Don't come up with your five cents' worth. Don't follow suggestions of this advisor or that advisor. Stay right there. By the dry brooks of life our God is water in a dry place. Our God can make a way out of no way. Our God will make a way somehow. All He wants is somebody to trust in Him.

Well, that's it. I wish I had a chance to ask if anybody reading this book has ever stood by a dry brook, if you've ever had it so rough that there wasn't even any dew, but somehow or other God refreshed your life. I'd love to hear your story of God's faithfulness. Because He is a soul reviver. He does refresh the soul. He does lift us up.

As we've prayed over and over from Psalm 23, "He leadeth me beside the still waters, He restoreth my soul." I've got some good news. Surely. Surely. "Surely goodness and mercy shall follow me all the days of my life."

6

---∞∞---

COURAGE TO FACE TOMORROW...
BECAUSE OF WHAT GOD DID YESTERDAY

David said, "Moreover, the LORD that delivered me out of the
paw of the lion, and out of the paw of the bear, he will deliver me
out of the hand of this Philistine."
And Saul said unto David, "Go, and the LORD be with thee."

1 SAMUEL 17:37

First Samuel 17 is the record of the confrontation between the Philistines, the people of Philistia, and the Israelites, the people of God. You will recall that they stood against one another on mountains, threatening war. You will recall that a suggestion was made that rather than have an all-out war they might pick a representative, a strong man, from each side and send the two of them to battle. Whichever side's representative won, that side would win. If the one Israel selected won, then Israel won. If the one the Philistines selected won, then the people of Philistia won. You will recall that it did not take long for the Philistines to select their representative. They selected a giant of a man—a tall, muscular, skillful warrior named Goliath. I'm sure he had fought his way up through the ranks to be considered among the Philistines as their representative.

Not so with Israel, especially after the Israelites heard who the Philistines had selected. When he was described, his height, his strength, his spear, and all his armor, cold chills ran up and down the spines of all the Israelites, for there was none to compare in stature and in warfare to Goliath.

So the people of God murmured and whimpered saying, "Who will go out to fight for us?" They went through the line of their heroes, and none would go out to fight. They went throughout the sons of Jesse, save one, and none would go out to fight. And then, possibly the most humiliating thing happened, and that is that the Philistines decided to mock the people of God. They said, "Where is your man? Where is the one who is to fight against us? Where is your representative? Who will come out against the Philistines, or will Israel, who represents a God reputed to have might and power, lose by default?"

They taunted and chanted toward the hills where the Israelites stood. "Send us a man. Send us your selection. Where is the representative of your God? Who among you will dare come forward and fight against us?" And Goliath, roaring and growling and mocking said, "Send out somebody to help Israel and to fight for Israel." The people of God did not have enough courage to fight Goliath. They lacked the freshness of remembering what God had done, thus it did not occur to them what God would do. When you lose from your memory banks what God has done, you will doubt what God will do. That's why we're devoting an entire chapter to the subject of *Courage to Face Tomorrow . . . Because of What God Did Yesterday.*

REHEARSING THE VICTORIES OF YESTERDAY

Satan is in the business of spoiling and tarnishing our fresh recollections of what God has done in the past. He robs us immediately, not letting us hold too long to the victories God has given us. He comes in swiftly with another problem or another sickness or another doubt or another fear. He comes in swiftly to try to knock out the fact that he was knocked out in the last round. He dances around us like he has won every round. He can recoup and regroup quicker than anybody I've ever met. You can smash him. You can bloody his nose. You can get up right in his face, and yet he will regroup and get up and fight you again.

He's a bugger. He's a mess. I'm talking about Satan. He can say you're not going to make it. He can tell you you're not going to have any food on your table and come to dinner at your expense. He's a bugger. And many church people need to learn how to keep a fresh account, an up-to-date account, a quick memory; you need to wire your computer, so that as soon as a challenge comes before you, you can hit the computer bank and it will bring forth the victories of yesterday and they will flood your mind to the extent that you will say to the Lord with fresh abandon, "Here am I."

Why was it that Israel wasn't the first one to go forward? Surely the God of Abraham, Isaac, and Jacob, surely the God of Egypt and the midnight raid of the death angel, surely the God of the flip-flopping of the sun, surely the God who led them across rivers and seas on dry land twice in their journey, surely the God who brought water out of a dry rock, surely the God who rained down manna from on high, surely the God who rained quail down from heaven's kitchen, surely the God who drove their enemies out from in front of them, surely He could handle this situation. But when you let circumstances in life overcrowd your mind so there is nothing in your mind but the present problem, you will freeze. If you don't let anything in your mind, except what you are facing now, then you'll freeze.

But if you can just open up your heart and rehearse the victories of yesterday, all the way back to when you were a child, you can make it.

You can hardly get me to be despondent, you can hardly get me to despair, because I'm too far ahead of where I ever thought I would be. Because of my log-cabin upbringing, it's easy to please me at hotels. The people say, "Is this room all right?" And there I am at the Hyatt and at the Stouffer and at the Sheraton and at the Hilton. And the people who have invited me have put me up in a suite, and they walk in and say, "Now, Reverend, is this all right?" My mind goes back to the log cabin, and that's what I compare it with. As a matter of fact, I don't feel quite comfortable in here because this is too much for me. The last time I was down in Alabama they gave me a suite, and I said, "Would you mind just cutting off the living room? This bedroom right here is enough for me." I never thought I would get one-fifth, one-eighth of where I am. So you can't make me despair. I mean, I now wear shirts I bought. And up until eighteen all of my shirts were given to me. I'm far down the road now.

PARALYSIS OF FEAR

And so the people of God stood with fear to the point of paralysis. There was no one to go for them. And you can hear it all in the camp of the Philistines. You can hear them laughing and scoffing. And there is silence from Israel's camp. And that's much like it's getting to be in our community. On every corner the dope pushers are saying, "Here we are. We are out of the closet. We don't care that you know we are pushing dope on your front yard." They are unashamed.

There was one warrior, however, that Israel had never considered. First of all, he was but a youth. He had no training. He had no experience with warfare as a soldier. He had never seen Goliath, but he came from having fed the sheep. He heard this giant of a man roaring, and he saw the fright in his own people. And he came and he said, "What on earth is going on? Who is this defying the army of the Lord?"

They said, "You see, since you were gone we worked out something. We're supposed to pick somebody to go out and fight."

And he said, "All right. Why isn't the fight already under-way?"

They said, "Come here. Let us show him to you, and here's his résumé if you want to see it."

And David said, "I still don't understand. What do height, muscles, and physique have to do with this matter? What does his ability to wield the sword and throw the spear have to do with fighting him?"

And they looked at him a little funny. "It has everything to do, because that's how you get killed, people wielding the sword and throwing the spear, breaking your neck with their muscles."

He said, "But you see, that's if you use the armor of man. It's according to what armor you select. According to how you're going to fight. You all must remember we are the people of God, and our God is the one who fights our battles. How have you so quickly forgotten that we did not dip our toes in Red Sea water, but we walked across on dry land? We did not kill a single member of Pharaoh's army, but God saw to it that they drowned. How quickly have you forgotten that God drove them out from before us? Don't you know our God is a God who can fight our battles?"

I'm sure, there were those who said, "Don't waste time with this kid. He's not familiar with these matters. He has a long way to come. He's a spiritual fanatic. He can't handle this matter."

But David said, "Don't push me off too quickly. I have

some things that I haven't been telling you all. I have some victories that I have not testified about. I can handle this matter." Out of that whole army of men, even yet were none willing to fight this battle. So the army, by consensus, let this boy suit up for battle.

King Saul said, "Well, if he must go, let's fix him up. Put our armor on him." Being an obedient child he let them put their armor on him. He let them cover him up with the mail and with the breastplate and put a sword in his hand.

Then he said, "Oh King, I don't want to be disobedient, but I never used any of this stuff before. This won't win. First of all, it won't win because it won't be me. I don't fight with this. I have a name that I fight with. I don't fight with swords. I have a name and a prayer. Secondly, if I went out and won with this, then all praises would go to your armor, your sword, and your spear. I would appreciate it if you would take this stuff off, but don't get fearful, because we've already won. Get the cheering squad ready. Get the banquet committee ready. Our God has already given this Philistine into my hand."

There was silence. There was sadness. There was a spirit of helplessness as a little sheepherder approached the giant. There was a hush in the army of the Lord. They were ashamed that they couldn't come up with anyone bigger than David—that they couldn't come up with anyone stronger than Goliath. They sat shivering, waiting for his body to be returned; yet they let him go.

There was shock and dismay on the Philistine side. There was laughter as they saw this twig of a boy approaching this giant, Goliath. "Look who Israel finally came up with. And he's coming out here with no spear. He's coming with no sword. He's coming with no shield." Then there was madness on the part of Goliath. He said, "What is this? I've never been so humiliated. I've never been so insulted. That somebody would come after me as if I were a dog. Let me chop this boy up in a hurry and take over the Israelite army."

But David said, "There is a difference. You come to me with your sword and your shield. You come to me with your military preparedness. But I come to you in the name—I have a name—of the God of Abraham, Isaac, and Jacob. And I'm going to take your head back to my king. I have a slingshot, and I don't need but one stone. Because the God I serve doesn't need rehearsal. He doesn't need to practice. He's able to put speed behind this rock. It's not by my might. I can't throw a rock that hard, but God is able to put speed behind this rock."

It isn't in there, but in my mind he said, "One for the Father, one for the Son, one for the Holy Ghost—because you know they're all One." He wound it up. He let it go, and God guided the rock past the shield, past the coat, and got that one spot that was uncovered. That rock hit the big old giant in the head, and he dropped dead. And this little boy that the Philistines were insulted by, this little boy that the Israelites doubted, stood, took the giant's sword, cut Goliath's head off and brought it back in the name of the Lord God.

Surely He Will Deliver Me

David said, "A few days ago a lion came up to the sheep, and I took my hand and smote the lion. A bear came to me. I took my hand and smote the bear." And David used the word that I can use myself, *surely.* "Surely, surely, surely the God who delivered me from the lion, who delivered me from the bear, He will, He *will* deliver me."

Is there anybody here who can say, *Surely?* Did He heal you? Surely. Did He save you? Surely. Did He deliver you? Surely. Did He take you off drugs? Did He take you off alcohol? Did He touch you? Then He will tomorrow, next week, next month, next year, He will. He will.

Consider the old hymn "God Will Take Care of You," written by Civilla D. Martin (1869–1948):

> *Be not dismayed whate'er betide,*
> *God will take care of you;*
> *Beneath His wings of love abide,*
> *God will take care of you.*

And I'd like to think young David's example inspired this last verse:

> *No matter what may be the test,*
> *God will take care of you;*
> *Lean, weary, one upon His breast,*
> *God will take care of you.*

> *God will take care of you,*
> *Through every day, o'er all the way;*
> *He will take care of you,*
> *God will take care of you.*

7

---○○○---

IF THE FOUNDATIONS BE DESTROYED. . .

If the foundations be destroyed, what can the righteous do?

PSALM 11:3

Y ou and I have lived long enough to know that we no longer need to ask the question *if* the foundations be destroyed. We are living in the age when many of the foundations *have been* (or are being) destroyed.

The things that made us great as a people and a nation, helping us build great institutions, establish great homes, rear productive children, and defend our country and much of the world are the very foundations being destroyed before our eyes in this generation.

Several years ago when I prepared my Youth Day message, I prayed and wrestled with the Lord to give me a special message for my teenagers. As they gathered in front of me, I realized I was probably not the best one to preach that message to them. My teenage life was so unlike theirs today; we had little in common.

I really couldn't relate to my teenagers, because I came out of a community of strong foundations. My spirit was always strong, because I lived in a community of strong foundations.

There was, first of all, the strong foundation in the home. When Poppa was living, those eleven years, we didn't have TV, but on his knees he taught me stories of good literature, and we had all that prime time together. After the sun went down we didn't have any lights, but we found things to do.

I was taught that I was a boy. I was taught that God had made me a male, and never was there a desire to be a female. I was taught that God made Adam and Eve; I was taught there was no third option. That was my strong foundation. But I'm living long enough now to see this strong foundation being tampered with, being brought down.

The youth of today don't have that strong foundation in our culture anymore. I was recently in San Francisco, where that city now has an arrogant boast that they are the capital of homosexuality. Thirty percent of the population declares they now have the alternative lifestyle. It's a city that is the cradle of that lifestyle.

Likewise, we're seeing in California that one out of two marriages end in some kind of separation. We're beginning to see articles in the newspaper claiming older adults should marry only with the consent of their children. We are seeing the foundation of the home being destroyed.

I came up in a community where there was never a locked door. We never had a key—couldn't even afford one. We only had a latch on the door, and that was to keep the wind from blowing it open. All we had to do was run down the road and tell a neighbor we'd be away from home for a while. While we were away, neighbors would bring in the mail, slop the hogs, feed our dogs and chickens, and see that everything was all right. When we'd return, the neighbor would come over and say, "There's an egg missing. One day a hen didn't lay, I don't want you to think I took it."

Our strong foundation of community fellowship is being destroyed. Not only do you need bars and locks, you don't tell the neighbor that you're away; you dare not, for fear he'll come over and rob you.

What Are the Righteous to Do?

The question comes in these days of crumbling foundations that you and I are forced to live and work in: What are the righteous to do? What kind of gospel are we to preach? What are we to say from the pulpits when we're living in an age of corruption, an age of crumbling foundations—the destruction of the home, the destruction of government, the destruction of righteousness, the destruction of strong biblical principles. Where are we to go, and what are we to say?

I lived in a community where we had one murder in the seventeen years that I lived there, and we wouldn't have had that if they'd paid attention to the preaching. We decided to have a rodeo one Sunday afternoon. The preacher was opposed to that, for he reminded everyone that Sunday ought to be kept holy. But we decided that if we went to church on Sunday God didn't have anything against a rodeo in the afternoon.

Then some boys came up from a community we called the low colony. They came up and got in a fight and shot one of our boys. That broke up bands and rodeos in Sweet Home even to this day.

So I came up in that kind of an age. Yet, I've lived long enough where just a short while ago in Los Angeles one of the leaders of our denomination stood and in agony delivered a message about his own disturbing doubts. He claimed that in our church there was a place for those who had doubts and questions. A place for those who don't quite know or who are not quite sure.

But I say, especially in these days of crumbling foundations, signals that are not sound and true have no place in our pulpits today. There are too many people just barely hanging on, too many people coming to our churches hanging onto a spider web as they float across hell. There must be no uncertain preaching, no uncertain preachers.

In these times when we can no longer look with exact certainty to the pulpit, we can no longer look to the schoolroom, we can no longer look at the family structure, we can no longer look at the mayor's office, the governor's office, the president's office; what are the righteous going to do?

Well, Psalm 11:1 says, "Flee as a bird to your mountain," get out of town, run. That's what it says to do. And that's what so many of us are tempted to do. So church members and non-church members have not fled to the mountains, but they do flee to their jobs. They talk to nobody, they go back to their apartments, they lock their doors, they put on the burglar alarms, they flee to their own places of safety.

But David takes exception to that advice, "How say ye to my soul, flee . . . ?" (Psalm 11:1). These are not times for us to flee. After all, there are no safe places to hide. You can move from Detroit to Florida hoping that you'll escape the pressures of the big city. In Florida you'll just run into alligators. No safe place. People ran from South Central Los Angeles running from the Negroes to Orange County. There they ran into the hippies. No safe place. They're now moving back downtown. No safe place. So He bids us not to flee, for there is no safe place.

A waitress down in Daytona Beach once said to me, "I don't have time to go to church. Besides that it's too dangerous to get out to go to church. So I have my church by my television at home." Well, I'm all for television ministries, but that's no substitute for assembling with a local congregation.

As Billy Graham says, "Find a Bible-believing church and go there and worship God." But even that is no substitute. What are we to do?

BE VERY SURE

These are times when the righteous must make their calling and election sure. Listen to 2 Peter 1:10: "Wherefore the rather, brethren, give diligence to make your calling and election sure: for if ye do these things, ye shall never fall." These are times when every one of us must spend time alone talking to God—making sure we've got it right between Him and ourselves.

Every so often when I fly to San Antonio, I fly on to Houston. I pick up a rental car, and I drive back down that highway ninety miles from San Antonio. Then I head nine miles into the dusty sand and into the mascot bushes to Sweet Home, the place of my youth. I get out of that car, and I walk across those fields where God says, "Talk to me." I stop at the exact spot where, when I was eleven years old, the Spirit of the Lord came upon me and said, "Preach my gospel." I remember how I ran until I was seventeen. I don't know how many lies I told God; I don't remember how many deals I tried to make with Him.

I go back to those places, and I cry. But I can cry in Sweet Home. Out there where I'm not pastor, where I am not known anymore. I get back there on that dusty road and I cry, but I always come away assured that God called me to preach. He assures me again that if He could take care of me in that log cabin with nobody but a man and a woman to help me, He can take care of me in the White House or my house.

In these days of crumbling foundations I suggest that every so often you do whatever you have to do to make sure you are sure your anchor holds. God knows you better than you know Him. He knows you need a double dose of His Spirit and faith in Him. Because in times like these you have to know that you know that you've been born again, for the tests will surely come.

In these days of the threat of nuclear war, with the threat of water running out, gas running out, power running out, somebody has to know he knows God and that He is still on the throne.

Back in Houston, when I was preaching at an auditorium where many white people would be, the police were there, too. The Ku Klux Klan put my name on their death list. When I looked at my little baby that they had threatened to kill, and my beloved wife who was also threatened, the only knowledge that kept me going was the fact that I knew God.

When I moved to Los Angeles, I refused to preach a black gospel (I refused to even use the word). I'm still a Negro. I'm proud of the fact that my great-grandfather was a Negro. I know that black is an adjective. And I'm not an adjective, I'm a noun; as a matter of fact, I'm a proper noun. You say black, you've got to say a black something, and it's that something that disturbs me.

When I refused to preach a black gospel, when I refused to deny my relationships with Billy Graham and Jerry Falwell, then I got another death notice. This time, not from the Ku Klux Klan but from the Black Panther Party. When they threatened my life, and when one preacher was killed, they put in the paper, "E. V. Hill is next." When they called me and said they'd be in my church next Sunday, and if I don't denounce this white man's religion, and talk about blackness, I'd never leave that auditorium.

You know, on Tuesday when the threat came I couldn't wait until Sunday. Not arrogantly or boasting, but I know that I know God. I don't know *of* Him, I *know* Him. I know He called me to preach. And He kept me safe.

Brothers and sisters, go home and tell everyone that in these days of crumbling and falling foundations, when even our flag is wavering over our capital, make sure that you are sure that you are saved.

OUR ULTIMATE PROTECTION IN A CRUMBLING WORLD

Ah, but there's another thing. Those who are sure they are sure must recognize that we cannot withstand the onslaught without putting on the whole armor of God.

We've got to get into Bible studies, we've got to get into biblical preaching, we've got to get into one-on-one counseling and discipleship, and growing as believers more than ever before. Because all around us there are humanists, feminists, communists, and homosexuals who make a quartet around and against every born-again believer.

They don't get up in church and challenge you on Sunday morning; they don't tell your preacher that he is preaching wrong. They are waiting for us all on Monday morning. Members are bullied and threatened when these militants get in control of departments in their various places of employment. They are lying in wait to get born-again Christians.

I have a boy in our church, an excellent master in business administration, who was fired because he refused a relationship with the homosexual head of his department. In the marketplace these are dangerous days. We must be equipped with the whole armor of Jesus Christ. We must wear not only the helmet of salvation, and the breastplate of righteousness, but the whole armor of God. We must be prepared. We must be fully equipped with the whole armor of God.

The devil is working in government and the home and the workplace. He is attacking everyone from the pews on Monday through Saturday. We've got to maintain the full armor even in our bedrooms. We must realize that the ship is under attack. All leaves are canceled. Since the devil is bombarding the church of God, we must put on the whole armor of God and prepare for duty. No time for ex–Sunday school teachers, no time for ex–prayer meeting attenders, no time for ex-witnesses, no time for ex-preachers. We need every soldier on deck, reporting for duty.

Do you realize there are eighty million of us who call ourselves evangelicals and there are countless other true believers who are not labeled evangelicals? They may not shout like my people do, they may not say "Amen" like my members do, but there are millions of them who can be counted among us.

With eighty million of us on the church rolls, why is it that our country is yet unsaved? In my church I have a committee that fits every background. I have an intellectual committee, so if you're a heavy thinker I put you on that committee. So when some youngster in high school claims he's read some book in some library and he's changed his mind about the virgin birth and about Jesus Christ, my intellectual committee comes to the rescue.

Then I have a committee on Jehovah's Witnesses. The girl who's chairman of that committee at one time taught the Jehovah's Witnesses how to teach. She heard the gospel, and I baptized her; now she teaches my members how to deal with the Witnesses and win them to Jesus Christ. So in our church, when the Jehovah's Witnesses come to a family's door and say, "Can we have a Bible study?" my folks say, "Oh, yes. May we invite a few of our friends, too?" Of course they say OK. Then the minute they leave, my members will call our Jehovah's Witnesses squad. At least one trained person commits to be in that meeting. When they believe they are in charge, this woman knows how to put the Blood on them. My group has gotten so good that now when a Witness calls on someone they first ask if they are members of Mount Zion Baptist Church.

I have a Black Muslim committee, and any time one of our boys begins to succumb to that teaching, I have two members of that committee who are former Black Muslims; they know what to do and say.

I have a committee that works with prostitutes. One Sunday morning a man came down and said, "I want to talk to you. I'm a pimp, and I've just been saved." He asked me what he should do. I told him I was not in the business of telling folks what they should do. I told him to ask the Lord what he should do.

The next Sunday morning there he was with four of his girls in the second row right beside him. They were clad with what they were used to wearing (they don't have church clothes). When I gave the invitation he told them, "Go down there and get yourselves saved." When it was all over I told him that's not the way you win people. He said, "You don't know a thing about prostitutes. I'm a pimp. Let me save prostitutes; you just go on and preach the gospel."

I was preaching for Dr. Criswell in Dallas some time ago. He said, "Brother Hill, I'm surprised. Do you mean that prostitution is a big business?"

I said, "Dr. Criswell, give me a day, and I'll bring you the statistics about it."

The next day I met a cab driver and asked him (for they will always know). He said they have at least three hundred pimps; each has from ten to fifty women. He said there were at least five thousand practicing prostitutes in town who must bring in at least two hundred dollars a night each. I'd call that big business.

All together, our church has dozens of committees that cover all phases of life, and they are making a difference in our community. Every member of every committee is ready and willing to report to duty. A man came down the aisle and said, "Preacher, I'm a drunkard; do you think God would save me?" Before I got a response out of my mouth one of my associate pastors said, "Let me have him, pastor."

Can a former prostitute stand up in your church and say, "I tricked for five years before I found the Lord, and now my ministry is leading prostitutes to Jesus"?

Report to duty. Get out of that pew and report to duty.

So, in these days of crumbling foundations make sure your anchor holds. Put on the whole armor; we've got to get out there. There's a world to save. Report to duty on the battlefield.

KEEP BELIEVING

Finally, in these days of crumbling foundations we must keep on believing. With all the weakness, cynicism, and sarcasm of this humanistic secular society, there's unbelief gradually rising in the hearts of people. Movies may just slightly misquote a Scripture, but it is enough to gradually put a question mark in the mind of the hearer.

You remember how Jesus was standing in the midst of a crowd and a woman touched the hem of His garment? You remember how in the midst of it all the runner came and said, "Don't bother, Master, she's already dead." The mourners had already assembled, the family was weeping. Remember what the Master said? "Keep on believing."

I don't care what the skeptics say. This is the Word of God. I still believe He was born of a virgin. I still believe He's the Son of God. I still believe God had only one Son, and that's Jesus Christ. And all other grounds are sinking sand. I believe that they crucified Him on Friday and that He died. I believe that early on Sunday morning He got up with all power in His hand.

Though it might look like the enemy is in control, I say, *KEEP ON BELIEVING.*

8

THE MODEL PRAYER

"After this manner therefore pray ye: Our Father which art in heaven, Hallowed be thy name. Thy kingdom come. Thy will be done in earth, as it is in heaven. Give us this day our daily bread. And forgive us our debts, as we forgive our debtors. And lead us not into temptation, but deliver us from evil: For thine is the kingdom, and the power, and the glory, for ever. Amen."

MATTHEW 6:9-13

This prayer is mistakenly called "The Lord's Prayer." It is not the Lord's prayer. John 17 would be more specifically called the prayer of the Lord Jesus. Matthew, instead, records the prayer that Jesus used to teach us how to pray. The disciples asked, "Lord, teach us to pray," and the Lord taught them with this model.

This is an important matter to be studied, taught, and preached in the church, because although we have the privilege to go to the throne of grace, we ought to follow the approach Jesus suggested.

Whenever you are going before some person of distinction, for instance, before you go to the White House, before you enter the Oval Office to meet the president, an official will first acquaint you with the proper protocol. What's right to say and what's not right to say.

It was my privilege some time ago to go to Tonga to preach at the eightieth birthday celebration of the king. It was necessary for me to learn the proper protocol—what to talk about, how to approach the king. They told me that every time the king bowed, I too should bow. Well, I told them that I couldn't do that, for the only person I bow to is the King of kings. They said, "The king understands that, but you have to be coached." I even needed to tell the officials beforehand what I would and would not do or say.

Now if that's necessary for an earthly mogul, how much more should we rehearse the proper way to approach the God of the universe?

To be sure, this isn't the only thing you can say in prayer, but this is the *model* prayer. If you were baking a cobbler, you'd follow the recipe. If you were sewing a dress, you'd follow the pattern. I certainly don't want to eat a cobbler made by someone who doesn't know the proper ingredients of a cobbler. And I wouldn't want my wife to wear a dress made without a pattern. How much more does this principle apply to prayer addressed to the Creator of the universe?

Approaching God is a simple matter. "Lord, have mercy," is a proper approach. "Help me, Jesus," is a prayer we sometimes have to pray. Sometimes when you can't remember the model, you just say, "Lord." This matter of prayer is just man talking to God. It's so phenomenal—it's hard to believe that God and I are on speaking terms. Have you ever thought about that? Some of you have never spoken to the mayor of the city, but you are completely able to speak to God.

It blows my mind that someone as sinful as I can go before the throne of God—and He hears me. That's wonderful. That's marvelous. The One who created the heavens and the earth is talking with a sinner such as I. I don't even have to worry about how many others are talking to Him at the same time. He doesn't have a party line.

He's so much God that He can hold a conversation with me right here, somebody in India right now, and somebody in Kenya right now. No matter how full the church is, God can hear every prayer that's uttered in the same instant.

THE PATTERN FOR PRAYER

Now, unlike some denominations that say this is the only thing we can say when we pray, that's not true. For this is just the model we should use to form our prayers. There are parts of this prayer that churches use that are not exactly like the original translation. Some translators even said, "I don't like this part." So they changed it. But this is generally like the original plan. This prayer is just the blueprint of what our language should be. You don't have to use it word for word. He just says, when you begin to pray, talk like this.

But just preceding that verse, Jesus tells us how not to pray. There are some people who are exhibitionists when it comes time to pray. They just rattle off word upon word, trying to sound pious and religious. Then they wonder why they get no answer.

You know, if we want to be effective, we have to have a pattern of prayer. I want you to know that this is the Lord's model prayer. So, if you don't know how to pray, follow Jesus' pattern.

KNOW WHO YOU'RE ADDRESSING

Now the first thing, when you come before God, like any noble, you say, "Our Father. . . ." There are lots of folks around

who will tell you differently, but the Book says, "Our Father.
. . ." If you get that far you're all right. First you're recognizing
Him as our and then recognizing Him as father. He's not "the
man upstairs," He's "Our Father." First of all, He ain't no man. I
wouldn't go to bed at night if I thought He was a "*man* upstairs."

To continue, the proper translation of the next is "who art
in heaven. . . ." That's His location. He wasn't Father Divine in
Philadelphia, or the guy down the street who calls himself God.
He wasn't the man called Jim Jones, who led so many to destruction. We've got to get higher than those. He's "Our Father,
who art in heaven." He's our heavenly Father. Though Heaven is
a long way from here, it's the backyard of our Father.

If you're very young, you wouldn't address an older person
by his or her first name. It would be Mr. or Mrs. If you're ad-
dressing a person of great distinction you'd use his or her title.
Likewise, we should approach God respectfully. "Our Father
who art in heaven. . . ."

Next take some time in recognition of His importance,
"Hallowed be thy Name." In other words, "Oh, how wonderful, glorious, marvelous is Thy Name."

So the first part of prayer is to realize who you're talking to.
Don't start out by saying, "I need this, I need that." You start
out by giving Him honor and praise. Spend a little time just
praising the Lord. "Bless the Lord, O my soul, and all that is
within me bless his holy name."

You just might want to say what the hymn writer of the
mid-twentieth century said: "How Great Thou Art."

O Lord My God! When I in awesome wonder
Consider all the *worlds Thy hands have made,
I see the stars, I hear the *rolling thunder,
Thy pow'r throughout the universe displayed:

Refrain:
Then sings my soul, My Savior God to Thee,
HOW GREAT THOU ART! HOW GREAT THOU ART!
Then sings my soul, My Savior God, to Thee.
HOW GREAT THOU ART! HOW GREAT THOU ART!

When through the woods and forest glades I wander
And hear the birds sing sweetly in the trees;
When I look down from lofty mountain grandeaur
And hear the brook and feel the gentle breeze:

And when I think that God, His Son not sparing,
Sent Him to die, I scarce can take it in;
That on the cross, my burden gladly bearing,
He bled and died to take away my sin:

When Christ shall come with shout of acclamation
And take me home, what joy shall fill my heart!
Then I shall bow in humble adoration
And there proclaim, my God, HOW GREAT THOU ART!

*Author's original words are "works" and "mighty."

BEING ON TIME TO MEET GOD

When I got down to Tonga, after flying about twelve hours, they met me at the airport. Then they took me to see the president. I said, "Your Honor, I'm deeply grateful for your invitation." Then he said to me, "I watch you on television every Sunday." Then he said, "We're glad to have you in Tonga—

please be seated." You wait for the invitation; you're never seated before he is.

I learned something else when I was down there. Our churches would do well to follow the example. Whenever there is a meeting the king is attending, it is unpardonable to be late. Everyone is in his seat fifteen minutes before his arrival.

At our church, we post a time of service. The sign says 11:00 A.M., yet some folks straggle in at 11:30. I think that's dishonoring the Lord. The Lord is in His holy temple, and you're expected to be in there in time to meet His arrival.

If you were God, and you were in heaven and people said, "Now come on and be with us, Lord," and you're looking down and seeing people standing in the parking lot, parking their cars, or across the street talking, or in the foyer gossiping, would you be impressed? Remember God's promise that when His people are gathered *together* there He will be in their midst (Matthew 18:20).

Suppose, instead, no one was finishing coffee or parking cars or in the foyer gossiping at 11:00 A.M. What if we were all in the sanctuary on our knees? I think the Lord would say, "I know they mean business."

Hallowed be His Name. We give Him high praise. When you go to see the mayor, when the mayor comes in, nobody asks you to stand. You would automatically show your respect by standing. When we say, "Let us all pray," and you're still looking around, the Holy Spirit looks down on that with disdain. Because hallowed is His Name.

PRAYING FOR HIS BUSINESS

Now the first thing, after we have acknowledged His holiness, after we have offered our praise, we pray, "Thy kingdom come, Thy will be done on earth as it is in heaven."

The next part in the Christian's prayer is for the work of the church. "Thy kingdom come." One of the problems we have in the world today is a crowd of churchgoers who are not kingdom conscious. They go to church by habit. But that's not a good enough reason to go to church. We ought to gather with the express purpose of seeing what else we can do to establish His kingdom on earth as it is in heaven. That's the purpose for being there. That's the purpose of going out into the world.

You go to a prayer meeting nowadays, it involves my sickness, my momma's sickness. Very seldom do you hear somebody praying for the advancement of the kingdom, for evangelism, for lost souls, for preachers who are standing in hard places. Your prayer is in proper order when you forget yourself and instead pray these words, "Thy kingdom come."

We ought to be praying that our cities and our country will be like the kingdom of heaven. We ought to be sick of the way that it is now. Just the other night, right down the street from our church where we were having a watch meeting, a bullet scraped the face of a young child. That ought to make us angry—that ought to drive us to prayer for God's kingdom to come on earth. Listen to every newscast; nearly every announcement is about somebody killing or robbing somebody.

But all is not that way in God's kingdom. It's peace in the kingdom. It's joy in the kingdom. It's there that the weary are at rest. That's why our prayers ought to be, "Thy kingdom come as it is in heaven."

We ought to start out by saying, "I want a *heavenly* home. I want my home like the kingdom." Start with the home. You wonder why there's not a church like the kingdom? It's because our homes are not like the kingdom. We have to have kingdom spirit in our homes and kingdom spirit in our hearts, if we want to have it in the church.

Too often, our number one reason for praying is "gimme."

But that's not in the model. The model prayer places praying for the kingdom first. Praying for a better church. More power in the preached Word. Praying that every member will come with heart and mind open. We ought to pray that our prayers would bring more sinners down the aisle.

ONE DAY AT A TIME

"And give us this day our *daily* bread." Jesus told us to pray for our daily portion. Don't make the assumption that you'll have enough for tomorrow. Don't make the assumption your job is going to last forever. Don't make the assumption you're going to live forever. Don't make the assumption nothing's going to happen to that which you have laid up.

There are a lot of people on skid row who have had better jobs than you have. But life is filled with pitfalls. You can have it today and have it be gone tomorrow. So learn how to pray, "Give me this day. . . ." This pattern gives you the latitude to pray for this day. You know what you need, and He will supply your need for "this day."

CONFESSION AND FORGIVENESS

Jesus continued in His model prayer, "And forgive us our debts." Ask for the forgiveness of your debts. Forgiveness of your sins. When you pray don't rush to "gimme," but confess and ask for forgiveness of your sins. If you can't remember them, develop the habit of writing them down.

Sit down, before you go to bed, and write down the things where you know you've done wrong today. Then confess them to the Lord. Then flush them away. Prayer should include the confession of your wrongs.

Then, He places here one of the most crippling statements

of Christian living. For He says, "As we forgive our debtors." This, my friend, is the condition of your forgiveness of your wrong. That is, you forgive those who have wronged you. If you don't forgive those, your Father will not forgive you for your transgressions against Him.

That means some of you have not been forgiven by God for many years. Are you one of those who, if you were honest, would say, "Yes, there's someone whom I haven't forgiven for a wrong committed years ago"? Here you are holding something against somebody else for twenty years. Or are you one of those who would say, "Oh, I've forgiven them, but I haven't forgotten them." You'd better be careful about that, for if you haven't forgotten, you can be pretty sure you haven't forgiven.

Thank God, when He forgives sin, He forgets sin. He drowns it in the sea of His forgetfulness, where it won't rise again.

THE ONE WHO DELIVERS

Now we come to probably the most overlooked portion of this model prayer. That is "and lead us not into temptation." Here is a little correction of the translation. It's not that God leads us to be tempted. It really means, "Help me to stay away from temptation," from places and things You know I can't handle. Keep me from that which would cause me to fall and go astray. Give me the strength to shun those things which would tempt me.

In my judgment, the most important part of this model prayer is, "And deliver us from evil." Here's what you're doing. First of all you are confessing that there's evil out there everywhere. There is evil out there because the evil one is out there. The devil is wherever you are. You can't go anywhere where evil is not. You can get up feeling holy and righteous, and before you turn around evil is there.

This prayer gives us an important part of what we should pray, "deliver us from evil." We know that we're not able to handle the devil, that's why we petition God to deliver us. Whatever it is that would cause us to yield to temptation, "deliver us."

A CLOSING BENEDICTION

Then Jesus said wrap up your prayer by letting God know why you are praying. You've made a whole lot of requests, now you know why, because He's got the whole world in His hands. "Thine is the kingdom, and the power, and the glory, forever."

Amen.

9

THE POWER OF GOD

He giveth power to the faint; and to them that have no might he increaseth strength. Even the youths shall faint and be weary, and the young men shall utterly fall: But they that wait upon the LORD shall renew their strength; they shall mount up with wings as eagles; they shall run, and not be weary; and they shall walk, and not faint.

ISAIAH 40:29-31

Way back in 1974, Christian leaders from across the globe gathered in Lausanne, Switzerland, for a conference on world evangelism. Billy Graham, in fact, preached the opening sermon for that conference. His message was on winning the lost at all costs.

The next night a gentleman from South America delivered a message not intentionally contradictory, but he claimed reaching the poor was the way to reach the lost. These two messages divided that great congress of 5000 delegates from 144 countries. Shall we win them or shall we feed them? This became the dividing question. You had to be a winner or a feeder—there was no middle ground. Third-World delegates and Negroes from the

United States, for the most part, took the position that you have to feed 'em. White evangelicals from the United States, for the most part, took the position that you must win 'em.

It was my responsibility at that conference to preach the closing sermon. You can understand the difficulty this provided.

The planners of the event started asking me for a copy of my message six months before. But I didn't have it then. In fact, even as I arrived in Switzerland I had twelve sermons in my briefcase but no specific message for the congress. God had not said anything. I have often been in that situation, and God has always brought a word at the right time.

The day before I preached, two delegations came to me. The one from the Third World and Negroes from the United States said, "Now Hill. Don't be no Uncle Tom. You know you are a brother, even though you run with white folks a lot, you are a brother. So you tell these white folks to feed 'em first. Because you know a hungry-belly baby can't receive salvation with its stomach hungry." Well, I know that not to be true, because I'm Example A that a hungry-belly baby can be saved.

And then the other delegation came, my beloved friends the white evangelicals and said, "Now, Dr. Hill, we have confidence in your theology, and we know you are going to tell them to win the lost at any cost."

So I stood up before a split audience. Either way I would go they would boo me. It was in that setting that God gave me a wonderful analogy to help define His purpose vividly in the hearts of both delegations. I had a great big screen behind me, and I asked a cartoonist to draw a diamond on it. My topic was the relevant church, which I compared with a baseball diamond.

What I said to those delegates at that conference is no less true today. Let me share with you some of those ideas in the hopes that you too will catch God's vision for a relevant, four-base church.

First Base Is Not Optional

The American national sport, baseball, requires that one hit the ball that the pitcher pitches and then run to first base before the ball can be picked up and thrown there by the opposing team. If a person makes it to first base safely, he or she is then expected to run from first base to second, from second to third, and finally from third to home plate.

Now there are some things you cannot do in baseball. You cannot score on first base. You cannot get to second base across the pitcher's mound. You cannot take a round trip to third base and score. You must touch first base first, then second, then third, and then home. It is only when you reach home plate that you have scored.

In the gospel there is a first base. First base in the gospel is reconciliation to God through Jesus Christ. The relevant church, the significant church, the church that's on target recognizes that there is a first base that we must get to, and we must get to it in a hurry. We can't play around. Even if you hit a home run you need to get on to first and touch it. I told that conference and I tell you, in studying the Bible carefully you will discover that first base is doing everything you can, with all of your might and all of your heart, to get people saved. That's first base.

Hungry belly, full belly, white, black, brown, rich, poor, inner city, suburbia—wherever you are, the number one issue is getting folks saved. In Matthew 6:33 Jesus says, "Seek ye first the kingdom of God, and his righteousness." In Luke 19:10 He says, "For the Son of man is come to seek and to save that which was lost." In John 20:21 the Master says, "As my Father hath sent me, even so send I you." And, as we've already seen in John 3 He declares in no uncertain terms, "Verily, verily, I say unto thee, except a man be born again, he cannot see the kingdom of God."

First base cleanses you, first base fills you, first base washes you, first base makes you love everybody. Praise His name. I know that's true, because I'm an example of how first base can give you a new heart.

The relevant church is the church whose everything—all that they have: singing, ushering, parking attendants, typists, preachers, evangelists, missionary society, baseball team—everything is moving toward getting people to accept Jesus Christ as their personal Savior.

At that point in my message my stock grew greatly with white evangelicals, but I went totally to the bottom with the Third World. But that's the Book.

I'm glad that I didn't have to choose between being saved and dying from starvation. I'm glad I got around to eating and being saved. But if I had to make my choice, I would really want to know that I'm saved. I hope that this nation will rise up and dignify itself and take every hungry person off the streets and every street person off the streets and put them in a warm place and feed them and clothe them. I hope that happens, but if we don't get around to doing all of that—save 'em. Get 'em saved.

At the church I pastor I have fifty-seven committees on winning the lost. I've already told you about some of them, including the ex-prostitute committee, the ex-pimp committee, and the Jehovah's Witnesses committee. Well, we have fifty-seven of these committees. Their methods differ, but their goal is the same: Save them. Save them. Work them in. Drag them in. Pull them by the hair (if they don't have wigs on). But get them in.

DON'T STOP AT FIRST, RUN RIGHT TO SECOND BASE

At that point in Lausanne, I had amens out of the driest Southern Baptists you would ever want to see. Then I said,

"Now wait a minute. When you get to first, you do not turn left, quit the game, go to the dugout and wait on the Rapture. First isn't all. Nobody scores from first base. There is no church that is relevant and significant if that's all it does. You have to do more. Once you have been genuinely saved you do not quit the game. You have to move on to second base.

Second base is where people who are reconciled to God form a visible brotherhood. Second base is where there is no east nor west, no north nor south. Second base is where the unbelieving world ought to look at our behavior and call us Christians. We have forty-seven committees in our church that address second base.

There are those who suggest this is really the only essential base. Thus, many try to get to second across the pitcher's mound, without going to first. But, in the words of Dr. Martin Luther King Jr., "You will not have strength to love or to form a brotherhood [on second], until you have had a genuine experience with God."

On second we must give evidence of salvation to the unbelieving world through the fruit of the Spirit. The world must now see a love so genuine. They must see a fellowship so pure. We haven't fed anybody yet, because the second need of the world is not food. It needs to see a demonstration of people who have been born again, manifested in effectuating a peace and a patience and a joy so different that the world says, "What on earth happened?"

Let me show you what I mean. A girl whose husband got converted at our church came out one Sunday night and walked down the aisle. I asked, "Are you coming down to accept Christ?"

She said, "No, I just want to know what has happened to my husband. He hasn't hit me in two days. He hasn't cussed me. What happened to him?" Somebody took her out and explained what had happened to him, and she came back in and accepted Christ.

A relevant church has a second-base movement that encourages love and fellowship and the manifestation of the fruit of the Spirit. The Holy Spirit *is* to make us love. He *is* to give us joy. He *is* to give us peace. He *is* to give us patience. He *is* to cause us to be longsuffering.

Someone might say, "Now, pastor, that's it. My church is making a hundred now, because we do everything to get people saved, and we really magnify love, joy, and fellowship. We have tea before the meeting, after the meeting, and late at night after that. We have coffeecake. We turn around and hug each other." But you're on second. You can't run over the pitcher's mound. There's a third base in this game, and you have to touch it.

THE TANGIBLE FAITH ON THIRD BASE

People reconciled to God and to each other must not hold hands on second until Jesus comes. We must proceed to third, where, motivated by Jesus' love, filled with agape, we seek to feed the hungry, clothe the naked, bind up the wounded, touch the untouched, heal the brokenhearted, free the captives of unjust circumstances and discrimination, bring close those who are far off, and shelter those without a home.

But do not stumble at this point as many have. For many have said that it is on third and third alone that we should concentrate all our efforts. Thus many churches and many preachers have emphasized the need of community improvement and community improvement alone. They tell us to ignore the gospel, (which requires personal repentance and personal acceptance of Jesus as Lord) and proceed to third and build there a utopia for man on earth. They say that if this is done, revolutions will cease and world peace will come.

If this were true, then Beverly Hills, California, would be the new heaven on earth. For in that city there are fabulous homes, streets of granite, flowers of beauty, skyscrapers, fabulous restaurants, excellent schools, golf courses and country clubs, no unemployment to amount to anything, and an average income that's off the charts. Yet, with huge incomes, with houses and land and silver and gold, that city has a psychiatrist, it seems, on every other corner.

Third base is where people who have been born again and who manifest it by the works of the Spirit are now ready to reveal community. I have forty-one committees in church for third base. Through these committees, we built the only highrise in Los Angeles where poor people can sleep in safety, people who have never lived in anything but community houses can have wall-to-wall carpet and draperies and brand new stoves and refrigerators. We have our own credit union where members do not have to be ripped off by loan sharks. We have our own blood bank, our own group purchasing and food purchasing co-op, our own clothing dispensary, even a Lord's Kitchen where everybody can get breakfast in the morning and supper in the evening for fifty cents if they have it. If they don't have it, they can be a guest of the Lord. That's third base.

But I don't want anybody working at third who hasn't been to first. I have people come and say, "We want to join your church because you help people, you clothe people, you feed people."

I say, "Don't join my church. Go to first base, pick up some salvation and go on to second and pick up some agape love, and then report to duty at third."

DON'T STOP UNTIL YOU'RE HOME

Somebody said, "Well that's where we ought to stop. Stop on third." No, that isn't a completely relevant church. Many people would say, "That's enough." But it isn't enough. You've got to tell people on third that you can't score until you go home, so you must write *temporary* on everything you see down here on this earth.

If you preach to me, tell me first of the need of personal salvation. Guide me to first base. Persuade me, through the teachings of the gospel to proceed to second and to discover the warm fellowship within the brotherhood of Christ. Then join hands with me to build a better community, but please don't leave me on third.

For a little while, houses and land will suffice. But, like Abraham, my soul looks for a city whose builder and maker is God. Don't leave me on third; take me home. For, no matter what we build on earth, no matter how firm our foundation, God has written *temporary* on all of them. They shall pass away. The gospel must have a home base. The gospel must tell all men that by and by they've got to go home. And there are only two places to go: hell or heaven. Heaven requires reservations; hell does not.

This is only my temporary headquarters. I want streets of gold. I want a land where the wicked cease troubling and the weary are at rest. I want a home where there is no more sickness or sorrow or death.

Because I've been to first base, I've got a home prepared where the saints abide together forever.

THE POWER TO RUN THE BASES

After hearing all this, I'm sure that you are overwhelmed. I don't blame you. The statistics overwhelm me. The needs overwhelm me. We all feel our own inadequacies. We know that within us there is neither strength nor resources, power nor knowledge to bring people around these bases. Indeed, our task makes our efforts look like grasshoppers. But we need not limit our plans to our strength.

There is a power that can change the minds of men. There is a power that can make enemies footstools and stumbling blocks turned into stepping-stones. There is a power that can make straight lines with a crooked stick. There is a power that can turn harlots into missionaries. There is a power that can turn cursing and swearing men into gospel preachers. There is a power that can open Red Seas, furnish manna from on high, cause walls to fall by marching. And there is a power that can confound the enemy on the battlefield. This power is available unto us. For He who has called us and sent us, has not, and will not, leave us. But rather, He is ready to empower us.

He promises that as we go there will be strength for today and courage for the battle. It was in the thick of the fight that the sun stood still. It was in the thick of the fight that the fire fell on Mount Carmel. It was in the thick of the fight that the Red Sea divided. It was in the thick of the fight that the prophet saw horses and chariots surrounding the enemy. Wait no longer! Look for no other sign! March now. Our God has spoken, and He says, "Move." Make plans equal to His strength, not ours. Let our vision be a challenge to God's resources, not ours. If we do so, the world will begin to see that in our God there is no end to His power.

I close with this powerful prophecy of Isaiah (40:28-31), spoken as inspired by God Himself:

Hast thou not known? Hast thou not heard, that the everlasting God, the LORD, the Creator of the ends of the earth, fainteth not, neither is weary? there is no searching of his understanding. He giveth power to the faint; and to them that have no might he increaseth strength. Even the youths shall faint and be weary, and the young men shall utterly fall:

*But they that wait upon the LORD shall renew their strength;
they shall mount up with wings as eagles; they shall run, and
not be weary; and they shall walk, and not faint.*

10

10

THE BURDEN
OF THE LORD

*"For God so loved the world, that he gave his only begotten Son,
that whosoever believeth in him should not perish, but have
everlasting life."*

JOHN 3:16

I want to discuss with you the burden that the Lord has. It does not sound theologically correct to suggest that God has a burden. Well, what burden is it that He would have, that He Himself is not the answer to? Without a long discourse I will simply tell you that God has a burden.

Now, the objective of most church people is not to be concerned with the burden of the Lord. Most church people are concerned with getting the Lord concerned about their burdens. Most church people are trying to get God's attention and get God involved in their needs, in their burdens, in their problems. Most of our efforts are centered around, "Lord get involved in what I'm involved in." Let me tell you, that's not right.

This principle became crystal clear to me one New Year's service when I pastored in Houston. That night Sister Stephens got up and said, "I want to give my New Year's determination."

I said, "All right, go ahead."

She said, "I'm determined this year not to ask the Lord to go with me anywhere." These words, coming from such a saintly woman, caused a murmur in the audience.

I said, "Now, Sister Stephens, would you say that over again? We didn't quite hear or, at least, didn't understand."

She said, "I said I'm not going to try to get the Lord to follow me nowhere and to go with me nowhere."

I said, "Sister Stephens that doesn't sound right, but—as the old folks say—'splain it to me."

And she said, "Well here it is. All these years I've been telling Him, come here, come there, go here. I've led Him into one mess after another. So this year I'm just saying, 'Lord, I'll follow You. I'm going to get up in the morning, and if You don't have anywhere to go I'm going back to bed.'" Imbedded in that folksy thought is a theological truism that our mission and our concern ought to be, first, what is the burden of the Lord? Does God have a concern? Is God worried about anything?

I know we have burdens. For some, it is personal illness, and we are at liberty to go to Him for that. For some it is lack of job, lack of money, lack of satisfaction, lack of peace, lack of housing, lack of this or lack of that. But Christians—mature Christians—must rise above looking out for our own interests.

If we don't watch ourselves, our interest in God will become wrapped up only in what God can do for us. But the Christian journey is not only what God provides for us, but it involves what we commit ourselves to doing for Him. And you can't do anything for Him until you learn what His burden is.

What can you do for God? Can you buy Him a suit? Since

heaven and earth are His footstool, how are you going to design a suit for Him? What jeweler in town can design a ring for God? Suppose we decided to give Him a ring. Who could make it, and where would he get the gold sufficient to make God a ring? So, then, what is the burden of the Lord that you and I should become involved in, obsessed with?

WHAT'S ON GOD'S HEART?

The burden of the Lord is the lostness of mankind. That's what God's main concern is. Not you getting a better job. Jesus would have never come all the way from heaven just to help you get a job. He has other ways. But He didn't come here for that. He didn't even come down here to pass out blessings. He wouldn't have had to go to Calvary to pass out blessings. He has angels and archangels who could have done that for Him. But He came because He was burdened by the lostness of mankind.

Remember John 3:16: "God so loved the world . . ." He had a burden that was so strong that rather than see man perish, He gave His only Son. Your lost son is the burden of the Lord. Your lost grandchild is the burden of the Lord. Your momma who's on the streets is the burden of the Lord.

What disturbs the Lord is that He can't get His church burdened with His burden. In this present age we are to work the works of Him that sent us while it is day, for "the night cometh, when no man can work" (John 9:4).

If the Lord sends you a blessing, you can be certain He didn't have you in mind as the end result. He's just trying to get it through you to somewhere else. And I want to tell you something, if He can get it *through* you, He'll send it to you. That's why He hasn't sent some people any blessings. They'd get it and build a dam and dam it up and can it up and sit on the can. But when God sends you a blessing, you have the responsibility of saying, "God, what do You want me to do with this?"

He's not interested in overcrowding your crowded closet. He's not interested in putting shelves in your over-shelved room. He's trying to reach some naked, homeless people. He's trying to reach sinners and lost persons. All of us must admit that we have been poor friends of God. We haven't passed it on. Negroes love to cuss white folks out for not passing it on. But we ain't so good at passing it on ourselves. When we get a nickel we'll hold it until the Indian hollers. We need to know how to pass it on.

TELLING THE LOST, WHEREVER THEY ARE

When you see a boy who's obviously involved in gang activity and wickedness, that's the burden of the Lord. When you see a tattered, torn woman who is obviously involved in elicit behavior, that's the burden of the Lord. When you see the homeless digging into trash cans, that's the burden of the Lord. When you meet a college professor who claims there is no God, that's the burden of the Lord. When you find a politician, that's the burden of the Lord. The Lord's not only burdened by the derelicts, the dropouts, the drug addicts, the prostitutes, the pimps, the poor folk and the homeless, He's also burdened by educated, highfalutin intellectuals and upstairs folk who claim there is no God. We have to witness at every level. Somebody must tell the drunkard, "You must be born again." But don't miss the mayor. She needs to be told, too. You must be born again. Somebody must tell the bad boy he must be born again; somebody must also tell the fraternities: the Alphas and the Sigmas, and everybody else. We must not only tell the obviously sinful folk that they need to be born again, but we must tell the Nicodemuses whose sins are not so obvious. Remember what we said earlier—it's true for everyone: "Verily, verily, truly, truly, you must be born again."

And this is the burden of the Lord. He's trying to get this nation not in first-class housing but saved. He's trying to get this nation not educated but saved. It would have been so marvelous if the president of the United States—and I recognize the ACLU wouldn't have let him do it—but when he said, "I want to be known as an educated president," it would have been wonderful if he could have said, "And I want to be known as a saved president." I know the Jews would have had a fit. I know the Arabs would have had a stomachache, but God would have smiled. I'd rather please God than everybody else.

You may be into a whole lot of stuff, thinking, "I wonder how so-and-so feels about . . . Did I impress my principal? Did my superintendent take note?" I tell you what you do: You let the audience be God. When God is pleased, He'll make these other folk your footstool.

A REAL-LIFE EXAMPLE

Now Hezekiah, king of Judah, is an example of one who sought the burden of the Lord. When he became king, he did not consider his desires. He came into the kingship knowing what God liked and what God didn't like. Listen to the way he is described in 2 Kings 18:1–7a:

> *Now it came to pass in the third year of Hoshea son of Elah king of Israel, that Hezekiah the son of Ahaz king of Judah began to reign. Twenty and five years old was he when he began to reign; and he reigned twenty and nine years in Jerusalem. His mother's name also was Abi, the daughter of Zachariah.*

And he did that which was right in the sight of the LORD, according to all that David his father did. He removed the high places, and brake the images, and cut down the groves, and brake in pieces the brazen serpent that Moses had made: for unto those days the children of Israel did burn incense to it: and he called it Nehushtan. He trusted in the LORD God of Israel; so that after him was none like him among all the kings of Judah, nor any that were before him. For he clave to the LORD, and departed not from following him, but kept his commandments, which the Lord commanded Moses. And the LORD was with him; and he prospered whithersoever he went forth.

He immediately started doing what God wanted done. He tore down the high places. He destroyed the idol statues. He destroyed the wicked worship. He got busy doing what God wanted him to do. I wish I could convince a couple hundred of you all to forget what you want and do what God wants. I wish you would tear up your most-wanted list and find out what God wants. I wish you would quit running around hunting for blessings and decide to be a blessing.

God's folk must not waste the time of grace searching out personal blessings. God's people must decide that the Lord saved us for a work, not a rest. Not a fabulous living, but a work. Hezekiah worked the work of God. This Scripture says he did everything that was right in the sight of God. It says God was pleased, and He caused him to prosper. That prosperity was not money in his pocket, but that prosperity was what enabled him to do more of God's work.

If you really want blessings, get wrapped up in the work of the Lord. If you want joy, save a soul. If you want joy, bring back a backslider. If you want joy, work the works of Him who sent you while it's day.

An Unlikely Turn of Events

He did everything right in the sight of God. And then we turn to chapter 20. Here is a man who's pleasing God. Here is a man who is working for God. Here is a man with whom God is pleased, and you open up with chapter 20 saying, "And he got sick."

But here is a man who God said did everything right. God said he was pleasing in His sight, and the first verse says, "And he took deadly sick." You got a whole lot of people saying, "If you walk in the will of God you won't get sick." Where are you coming from? There are people in hospitals and convalescent homes who are better Christians by nature than you are on purpose. You can't strut around and act like you haven't done anything wrong and that's why you've got your health. You got your health because God rains on the just and the unjust. You have your health because He's just that way.

And so Hezekiah took sick and Isaiah said, "Get your house in order, because you're going to die." But then Hezekiah turned his face to the wall and he said, "Lord, I have received the information that I'm going to die, but I just want to remind You that I have done Your will. I worked for You. I tore down the high places. I labored in Your name. I did everything that I thought You would want done. Now here I am sick unto death."

The Lord said, "Isaiah, go back to him and tell him I've heard his prayer. I have seen his tears, and I've added fifteen more years to his life. Don't worry about dying for fifteen years. Don't worry when you get a pain; it won't bother you for fifteen years."

And then Hezekiah said, "How do I know that this is real?"

And Isaiah said, "What sign do you want? Do you want God to let the shadow go down ten degrees?"

And Hezekiah said, "No, that could happen even if clouds overcome it. But I tell you what, let that shadow go backward, and then if it's really God speaking ask Him to bring that shadow right on back up."

And Isaiah said, "So it is."

When you're dealing with God, whatever your needs are while you're working, so it is. Whatever you come up against, so it is. He can divide the Red Sea, give manna from on high, heal the sick, regulate the mind, fix the heart, rejoice your soul. He can make a way out of no way. He can fight your battles if you just keep still. He can.

But if you work, work for Him and forget about yourself. Labor. Give your tithes. Give your offering. Then forget about it. I'm a living witness God will take care of you. God will see you through. God will give you strength. It pays to serve Jesus. It pays every step of the way.

11

THE BIG ONE

For the Lord Himself shall descend from heaven with a shout, with the voice of the archangel, and with the trump of God: and the dead in Christ shall rise first: Then we which are alive and remain shall be caught up together with them in the clouds, to meet the Lord in the air: and so shall we ever be with the Lord.

1 THESSALONIANS 4:16-17

For the Lamb which is in the midst of the throne shall feed them, and shall lead them unto living fountains of waters: and God shall wipe away all tears from their eyes.

REVELATION 7:17

There is a strange unity in the minds of even the unfaithful that the world is on the verge of something destructive, and it is near. You can see it in our comics; impending doom is the thesis of the average television viewing. Both saints and sinners, laymen and scientists, speculate that we're on the verge of the big one.

The big one. Devastating. Totally destructive. Something that's about to destroy what is known as our present civilization. It is, in the minds of most people, imminent. There is no longer a question whether or not we're going to suffer tragedy. Most people will concede that one way or the other, mankind is facing destruction. It used to be only the so-called religious persons. Only the old-fashioned preacher was expected to cry out, time that has been will be no more.

To be sure, all of the times of the past, there have come scoffers who have scoffed at the idea that anything was going to happen to this world. There have been those who have believed that this world was going to be an unending journey of one generation after another. There are those who just several decades ago believed that we had inexhaustible resources—an everlasting supply of natural resources. That there was no such thing as winding down.

But we have lived long enough now to see on the horizon the fulfillment of the prophecy of the prophets of old. For we're running out of gas, we're running out of oil, we're running out of pure water, we're running out of fresh air. Even the most optimistic person feels there is a big one coming.

However, there is much debate over what, who, or how the big one will come, and what it will be. That's why I've taken on that discussion with you.

MANY THEORIES

Some scientists have surmised that there is a frigid period coming, saying that much of the world will be frozen and that man will be decimated. These fears are confirmed by viewers of telescopes and readers of scientific data. They believe that the big one will be an ice age.

So some people may think they can survive this frigid period by fleeing the north and going west. But those who go toward Iowa and Nebraska, Oklahoma, and the Texas panhandle will find themselves in the dust bowl where the destruction could come from the great dry. There are those who suggest the big one is going to be ongoing drought.

There are those who have left the east coast and those who

have left the dust bowl and have come to the Sunbelt. But in the Sunbelt, where once there were lush green fields and wild life scurrying everywhere, there are now high-rises—condos and huge office buildings. There are those who suggest if you're not killed by the ice, or the dust, you'll not survive the over-growth of population.

Then there are those who have decided they've had enough of the cold, and enough of the dust, and enough of the hazards of the Sunbelt, and they've moved to California—only to be rocked out of their beds by earthquakes. In Nevada, away from California they are selling "beachfront property," convinced that California is going to drop into the ocean and Nevada will be on the beach. There are people who fervently believe the San Andreas Fault will rock and that California will fall into the ocean.

Twenty-two million have fled California fearing they might fall off into the ocean from the big one. There are those who declare that will be the big one. Be assured that would be a big one, but that will not be *the* big one.

If all the fears that move Americans from place to place are true, it would certainly be a big one, but it's not *the* big one.

There are those who declare that nuclear destruction will be the big one. We're in a position to destroy Russia a hundred times over, and Russia is in a similar position, that it could destroy us. Many countries are building and stockpiling nuclear warheads. One man could have a bad dream and touch the wrong button, and the world as we know it would be annihilated.

There are people who are building shelters under homes and stockpiling supplies to prepare for such an occurrence. They fear that vegetation will be destroyed so food will not be available. They've got machine guns so they can shoot down anyone who might try to invade their hideouts.

But I have a home already prepared. I don't have to hang

on to this earthly house, a place not made with hands. I'd rather be there than shooting my neighbor over a piece of bread. I'd rather be there where the wicked cannot invade, where the weary are at perfect rest. So the wicked are preparing for a nuclear holocaust, and I warn you, that is a real possibility. Because if an atomic bomb is getting into the hands of small powers, such as Iraq, Iran, North Korea, Israel, or other smaller nations, it could well happen.

If Hitler had had a nuclear warhead, he would not have hesitated to use it. Even though our fears about the small countries is real, I can tell you for sure, it is not the big one. It may be a big one but it's not *the* big one.

THE WORLDWIDE *BIG ONE*

The big one will be universal. It will happen to everybody, everywhere. It'll happen on the east coast and the west coast. When the big one comes, there'll be no need to run for shelter. There'll be no hiding place. I say to you, get ready for the big one. Moving from town to town won't get you ready.

When the Lord gets ready, you can't run. When the big one comes, it will be the same for the rich and the poor, the high and mighty, and the low and lowly. When the big one comes there will be no need to hide: it's going to reach you whoever you are.

So the real question is: Are you ready for the big one?

Paul tells us what the big one will be. He says, (1 Thessalonians 4:16-17) "For the Lord Himself shall descend from heaven with a shout, with the voice of an archangel, and with the trump of God: and the dead in Christ shall rise first: Then we which are alive and remain shall be caught up together with them in the clouds, to meet the Lord in the air: and so shall we ever be with the Lord."

One of these days He's coming back, and that's the beginning of the big one. The big one will begin with the rapture of the church. Oh, don't be left behind, for those who are will go through great tribulation.

Be ready for that "great getting-up morning." Be ready for the big one. Be saved. Be born again. Be working for Jesus every day and in every way. Be spreading the Word joyfully. Be praying expectantly. Be running the bases to get others into the kingdom. And most of all, be ready. I said, "Be ready!"

APPENDIX 1:
A MEMORIAL MESSAGE

"The LORD gave, and the LORD hath taken away; blessed be the name of the LORD."

JOB 1:21

The Lord gave, and the Lord hath taken away. I realize that this is a controversial text. Many say that the Lord gave, but they say it's not right to say that the Lord takes away. They say that the Lord does in fact give, but the devil takes away. They say that according to the Scriptures, the devil has come to steal and to kill. But the Bible doesn't say he will do it, it says he came to do it. If you don't have a shepherd, he will do it. But if the Lord is your shepherd, the devil isn't able to do to you whatever he wants.

The devil has to get permission to test me, he can't just walk up to me and take my life. My life is not in the hands of Satan. He doesn't have that power. If he did, all of us would be dead before nightfall. He's not going to let a host of believers like us live, if he has death in his hands. The Scriptures tell me that Jesus said, "[I] have the keys of hell and of death" (Revelation1:18).

THE GIFT BABY WAS

Job said the Lord gave and the Lord took away. In my life He gave a great gift. She was a gift, my wife Jane Edna Carruthers Hill (I called her Baby). Baby's father was a distinguished man. He earned his Ph.D. from Cornell University in 1920. Her mother was secretary to Felton Crofts at Southern University in Baton Rouge. She also was secretary to the lady who organized Phillis Wheatley homes throughout America. My wife was well-bred.

The Lord gave. He gave to Dr. and Mrs. John Carruthers a sweet child. Baby honored her parents. She loved them dearly. She labored at the bedside of her father until his death. She kept her mother in her home until death. She made her mother's last days her best days. The Lord gave.

She was never any trouble to her parents. The Lord gave in Baby a great student. She was trained in the best schools. Born on a university campus in Pineville, Arkansas; reared on the Furview University campus; she was exposed to great minds and personalities. She had the best in rearing and in culture.

She aspired to become a feminist woman. She was never aggressive and never said that she should be elected to anything. But quietly with a feminine approach she filled up two churches in one day, saying something to women. Her message was "You don't have to get out and fight, you might already be what God made you to be."

She did not come to what she was by accident; she studied culture and refinement. Her greatest desire was always to be appropriate. She would often come to my bedside before going to Bible study and say, "Do I look all right?" She would ask, "Am I pretty?" I had to say the day I saw her empty shell at the funeral home, "You're pretty, you're classy, you're a lady."

She studied and read classic literature. She was an extremist in what was proper. Extreme without being showy.

She accepted Jesus Christ as her Savior and the Bible as her guide in all truth. God gave our family a great woman. She was determined to be the best moral, spiritual, physically clean, and appropriate woman ever given to a man.

From childhood, she wanted nothing to be spotted on her. She wanted to save herself, to give herself to a man. So on August 29th, 1955, I received the wife only God could give. I only wish that I could have been half as good as the woman I married.

THE LORD KNEW WHAT HE WAS DOING

Our children had the tutelage of a prepared, loving, educated woman to bring them up. Our daughter Rose is now a practicing attorney; her husband is also. Our son Edward is pastor of Calvary Temple (Pentecostal Holiness Church) of North Hollywood.

In my wife the Lord gave my ministry a sure support, unwavering with never a controversy. She was my best friend. She was my greatest fan. No matter who preached, she'd say, "But they didn't preach it like you preached it." She was my greatest defender. When she had to work, she worked in hospitals and University Meds.

The Lord gave me an encourager. Once I invested in a service station in Houston. In that venture I lost my shirt. My wife, in one of those rare moments, said to me, before the station, "I wouldn't put any money in that; you've got too much else to do." I insisted, and she said, "Then go right ahead."

When I lost it, I called her and said, "I've lost the station." When I got home she wasn't at the door like always before. I thought, *Aha, she's pouting because we lost this money.* So I said, "Baby, where are you?" And she said, "I'll be out in a bit." I thought, *She's trying to say she told me so.* She finally came out, and I said, "Now, what's wrong?" And she said, "I've been figuring out." I said, "What have you been figuring?" She answered, "I've been figuring out that you don't smoke and you don't drink. And if you smoked and drank you would have lost about what you've just lost in the service station. So, six of one, half a dozen of the other. Let's forget it." The Lord gave.

I went home one evening when we were first married, and there were two places set and candles on the table. She said, "We've been married six months, and I thought we'd have a candlelight supper in celebration." That sounded groovy to me. But I went in the bathroom and turned the switch and no light came on. I went out and said, "Baby, did they cut the lights off?" She began to cry. She said, "You work so hard, and we're trying, but I didn't have quite enough money to pay the light bill. But I didn't want you to know about it, so I thought we'd just eat by candlelight."

She could have said, "I've never been in this shape before." She could have said, "I was reared in the home of Dr. Carruthers, and we've never had our lights cut off." She could have said, "I should have married the young fellow whose father was the president of Chile." (He was my brother-in-law's roommate in college. He fell in love with my wife. He said, "Come on back to Chile where my father is president." But she turned him down. She could have said, "In Chile our lights would be on.")

But she didn't say it. She could have broken my spirit. She could have demoralized me. But instead she said, "Let's eat by candlelight." She was surely my protector.

One night when I received a notice that I would be killed the next day, I woke up thankful to be alive, but I noticed she was gone. I looked out the window, and my car was gone. When she drove up, she said, "It occurred to me that they might have put a bomb in the car last night. If you had gotten in there you would have been blown away. So I got up and drove it, and everything is OK." The Lord gave.

She did not require a fur coat, just a simple dress. She did not require a Mercedes Benz, just a simple Ford. She never pushed; she never contended. Her words were, "My children and my husband are all right, I'm all right."

The Lord gave to Mount Zion a great woman. A great encourager. The Lord gave to this community a good citizen. I could go on and on because, so far as my wife was concerned, I could say I was one of the richest men on earth.

THE LORD TAKES AWAY

It is because of having been given so much in Baby that the rest of the text seems out of order. Having my life graced by such a wonderful person as Baby, I have a hard time dealing with the rest of that Scripture. We get so used to "morning by morning new mercies I see." We get so used to having all that our hearts desire. So we tend to stop at: The Lord gave. We take it for granted. So when the Lord takes away, we can't deal with that.

It's just like when you keep giving a child cookies and candies and ice cream, and everything else his heart desires. Then one morning you withhold it from him, and he falls on the floor and throws a tantrum. Because momma gave, and now she takes away.

When the Lord gives, when He rains down blessings, bless Him. But when He takes away, when He breaks your heart, when He doesn't give you what you ask for, can you still bless Him?

BLESSED BE THE NAME OF THE LORD

My text not only provides the explanation for Baby's death, but it provides the proper response: "Blessed be the name of the Lord." When her illness became serious, and when the doctors in private conference said they had done all they could do, I thanked them for their services. When my own doctor said he regretted he could do no more, I said, "You're a practicing physician, you're only practicing." Then I went into the chapel and said, "God, I want to talk with you. I want you to permit me to speak to you as I am. I'm an ignorant man, I don't really know how to talk to you, you're God. If you were a mayor I could talk to you. If you were a governor, I could talk to you, if you were the president of the United States I could talk to you (like I've already talked to some), but you're God." I said, "I want her back, and yet, my love for her says, let her go."

When I got through talking to God two words came into my spirit. Just two simple words, "Trust Me." Now I quickly concluded this meant He was going to heal her. But the Spirit did not say that. The Spirit said, "Trust Me." What He meant was that He might take her. Even then, I should be able to trust Him, even with Baby out of my sight. Trust acknowledges that He knows best.

In my sorrow, I had to read over the Scriptures that answer the question: What does He do with those He takes? What happens to them when the Lord takes them? What happens to Christians who die when you and I remain? Though they are no longer with us for they are absent from the body, they are with Him. "Absent from the body but present with the Lord" (author's paraphrase of 2 Corinthians 5:8). This corruption must take place in order that the incorruptible might take over. "Trust Me, I've got to pull out in order to put in. Trust Me." He tells me that He came for her and that I have to trust Him.

"This mortal must put on immortality" (author's paraphrase of 1 Corinthians 15:53). Death must be conquered. Trust Him.

The Bible says the keys of death, hell, and the grave are in His hands (Revelation 1:18). The Bible says this world is nothing to compare to the glory that He has prepared for us who trust Jesus. In 1 Corinthians 2:9, Paul writes, "But as it is written, Eye hath not seen, nor ear heard, neither have entered into the heart of man, the things which God hath prepared for them that love him." God says to me, "Hill, you think she is pretty, but just wait until you see her again. Just wait until I get her out of this earthen vessel and put her into her heavenly body."

In 1 Corinthians 15:52 Paul says, "In a moment, in the twinkling of an eye, at the last trump: for the trumpet shall sound, and the dead shall be raised incorruptible, and we shall be changed."

Just wait until the day that the dead in Christ shall rise. Just wait until Jesus himself shall descend with a shout, and with the trump, and the voice of the archangel. Just wait until we all see that house not made with hands but made to last eternally by our Father in Heaven.

I say, "Just wait. Just wait."

APPENDIX 2:
BIOGRAPHICAL SKETCH OF EDWARD VICTOR HILL

Edward Victor Hill was born in Columbus, Texas, on November 11, 1933. His parents were William and Rosa Hill. He spent his early years in Austin and Sweet Home Community, Seguin, Texas.

He accepted the Lord as his Savior on December 14, 1944, under the preaching of the Reverend Mayes at the Sweet Home Baptist Church. He was baptized in Reverend Rainey's tank and united with the Sweet Home Baptist Church at that time.

In his early youth he went to live with Aaron and Ella Langdon. He worked his way through high school as a hired hand, chopping and picking cotton, peanuts, and corn on various farms. He also made the fires for the church he attended.

Hill was active in the church. He was children's and youth choir leader, leader in the youth group, and active in every aspect of the church.

As a student in Sweet Home school, he was involved in sports, public speaking, 4-H, and New Farmers of America. He won many local, district, and state speaking, judging, and essay contests.

He was honored by the state of Texas for his work as a 4-H Club member in soil and water conservation. His efforts won him over seventy-five medals, certificates, and ribbons. His highest honor was raising the Grand Champion hog of the State Fair of Texas in 1947. He became the first Negro to receive the same price for his hog as did white boys, which was three dollars a pound.

While in junior and senior high school he was president of the Sweet Home student body and president of Area Three New Farmers of America. In addition he was vice president of the state New Farmers of America and president of the regional 4-H Club. He was also president of local, district, and state Baptist youth organizations.

Upon graduation from Sweet Home High School, he was awarded a four-year Jessie Jones Scholarship to attend the Prairie View (Texas) College, which he entered in fall 1951, majoring in agronomy. He was class reporter of his freshman class. In addition, he was president of the New Farmer's class and leader of the National Baptist Student Union. He was preacher for the Tuesday night prayer meeting that averaged 1100 students each week.

He received his call to preach in 1951 and soon after was licensed. He was ordained as a Baptist minister on December 29, 1954, by the Greater Mount Zion Missionary Baptist Church in Austin, Texas, of which Reverend J. H. Washington was pastor. He received his first call to pastor the Friendly Will Missionary Baptist Church in Austin, Texas, in 1954. He was also director of youth of the General Baptist Convention in Texas. Listed among "Who's Who In American Colleges and Universities In America," he graduated in 1955 among the top ten.

In 1955 he became pastor of the Mount Corinth Missionary Baptist Church of Houston, one of Houston's oldest and most prestigious congregations. He was twenty-one and single. But that soon changed when he married Jane Edna Carruthers, daughter of Dr. John and Susie Carruthers, in Prairie View, Texas, on August 29, 1955.

Through his pastorate there he led the congregation into becoming one of the most influential congregations in the state. The membership grew from 214 to 1100 active members in six years. The church was known to have one of the largest youth groups in America. Through his leadership, his church came into full participation in social, political, and civic endeavors. When the NAACP was outlawed in Texas, through Mount Corinth, Pastor Hill organized the Freedom Fund of Texas.

While pastoring Mount Corinth, Pastor Hill was an original board member of the Southern Christian Leadership Conference and nominated Dr. Martin Luther King as president.

Besides his office as pastor, he also served on local, statewide, and national boards. He was on the executive committee of the Baptist World Youth Conference in 1956. He served as a board member of the NAACP of Houston and the Negro Chamber of Commerce of Houston. Hill organized and was executive director of the Master Handicapped Workers of Texas, and was an active Democrat. He was an activist in more causes than there is room to enumerate. Worthy of mention is the awarding of an honorary Doctor of Laws degree by Union Baptist Theological Seminary of Houston.

On the first Sunday in 1961, Dr. Hill became pastor of the historic Mount Zion Missionary Baptist Church of Los Angeles, one of the oldest and most influential churches. The church was organized in 1892, with the peaceful exodus from the Second Baptist Church, to better serve the interests of the southern constituents.

During his tenure as pastor he has inaugurated many changes. First he suspended all the organizations and officers. Then he methodically reorganized the structure of the church based on biblical principles. When he arrived, the church was facing foreclosure. Within six months every note was paid. There were also $151,000 of lawsuits pending, which he settled within three months. The church property was refurbished, and two additional lots were purchased. The complete remodeling of the sanctuary was accomplished at a cost of $200,000, a great sum at that time. It is well-known as a missionary-giving church, donating thousands of dollars to various missions projects throughout the world every year.

Dr. Hill and his wife, during the thirty-two years of their marriage, raised two children, Norva Rose Hill Kennard and Edward Victor Hill II. They also have five grandsons and one granddaughter.

In 1987 Dr. Hill's beloved wife, Jane Edna, whom he called Baby, went home to be with the Lord. After four years of being alone, Hill was remarried to LaDean Donald, on March 7, 1992.

Throughout the years, Pastor Hill has preached the uncompromising gospel of Jesus Christ and maintains a high level of gospel presented from the pulpit of the Mount Zion Baptist Church. He has received over ten thousand people who have come down the aisles committing or recommitting themselves to Christ. He has baptized into the fellowship of the church over three thousand people who have confessed the Lord as Savior. Through his evangelistic fervor he has seen over twenty-five thousand people throughout the United States accept Christ as their Savior.

Dr. Hill has maintained a strenuous schedule of preaching and teaching for conventions, universities, colleges, seminaries, Bible conferences, local churches, and citywide revivals throughout the world. He receives an average of two hundred invitations per year, which keep him out of the pulpit of Mount Zion approximately twenty-four Sundays every year.

To recount all of his accomplishments and involvements in the religious and secular fields would take more pages than this book could hold. Dr. Edward Victor Hill has distinguished himself as a warrior of the faith and has been used of God in remarkable ways.

EPILOGUE

Dr. Edward Victor Hill did indeed have a home already prepared—and after running life's final base, he was ready for the last shout of *Victory in Jesus!* With arms stretched high in the victor's pose, he marched across heaven's threshold on February 24, 2003 after being stricken with pneumonia. His passing has thrust the Los Angeles church community and the national evangelical community into mourning.

In both communities there were few who hadn't come to know the name of the 69-year old pastor, who was the mainstay on the TBN network with his weekly TV broadcasts, a popular pastor and leading advocate on issues pertaining to the Los Angeles African-American community, and a sought-after speaker on the national evangelistic circuit.

What follows is his life story—a story of one who has run the bases well.

Edward Victor Hill was born on November 11, 1933, in Columbus, Texas, to William and Rosa Hill. He was reared in a log cabin by Poppa Aaron and Momma Ella Langram in the Sweet Home community near Sequin, Texas. He was born again on December 14, 1944.

He was married to Jane Edna Carruthers on August 29, 1955. To this union, two children were born. She preceded him in death on October 29, 1987. He married LaDean Donald on March 7, 1992.

Dr. Hill accepted the call to preach the Gospel of Jesus Christ in 1951 and in the same year, he was elected president of the Youth Auxiliary, National Baptist Convention of America, Inc. He was called to pastor his first church, the Friendly Will Missionary Baptist Church in Austin, Texas, in 1954. He attended Prairie View College and graduated with a Bachelor of Science degree in Agronomy in 1955. At the age of twenty-one, he was called to pastor the Mount Corinth Baptist Church of Houston, Texas. While there, the church grew to become one of the most influential congregations in Texas.

On the first Sunday in 1961, Dr. Hill took charge as pastor of the historical Mount Zion Missionary Baptist Church in Los Angeles where he remained the beloved pastor for forty-two years. He was a world-renowned evangelist, much loved but often criticized for his unswerving dedication to biblical correctness. He was considered one of the most significant preachers of the twentieth century. He set his face like flint, armed himself with the Gospel, and marched across the boundary lines of race, religion, denomination, and political preferences. Throngs of every bent received him. He was among the first Negro Baptists to preach on the Trinity Broadcasting Network, which began a love relationship that endured for decades.

When apartheid fell in South Africa, Pastor Hill preached one of the first messages aired on their Christian Television broadcast. So overwhelming was the call-in response that two secular newspapers reported, "the entire telephone circuitry shut down due to the overload. The capacity was ten thousand calls per hour, sixty thousand people called for prayer."

His message was sound and sure. His heart was as big as the

world. Everyone knew that his compassion was toward those who were in the lowest rung of society. His mind was as swift as lightning. His voice thundered with righteousness, punctuating the high points of his sermons. He was armed like a defense attorney with a reason for his faith. And the listeners were going to hear at least three reasons for faith in Christ in every sermon.

Mount Zion is a church where the poor can beg alms at the gates and be fed and clothed. In fact, after leading the church to purchase land, obtaining the building plans, and raising the money for a new church location, Pastor Hill was so moved with compassion for the growing numbers of hungry and homeless of South Central Los Angeles, that he asked the congregation to delay the new church to build The Lord's Kitchen. Over two million meals have been served to the needy free of charge. The Lord's Kitchen serves an average of two thousand meals a week and supplies other church pantries and feeding programs.

Pastor Hill's works, religious, social, and civic affiliations are legion. However, he was particularly fond of the fraternity of preachers of the National Baptist Convention, U.S.A., Inc. He deferred his opportunity to become president of the Convention to support a senior statesman for whom he had great respect. Years later, and in ill health, he ran unsuccessfully for president.

He has ordained and sent out to the nation over 1,454 preaching sons of Zion, including his namesake, Edward Victor Hill, II. He authored two books. *A Savior Worth Having* is a collection of life changing sermons that he delivered over his fifty-two years as a preacher. *Victory in Jesus* was in final pages when God called His servant home.

On Monday night, February 24, TBN aired one of Pastor Hill's sermons entitled "How to Cope." An hour after the sermon aired, Pastor Hill went into the presence of our Lord and

Savior Jesus Christ. It was reported that there were over one million viewers, which was one of the largest audiences ever. What an awesome, beautiful, picture of God's grace! On one side over a million believers being encouraged by the words of this man of God—on the other side an untold number joining their voices in a chorus of, "Victory! Victory! Victory in Jesus!"—as he crossed life's final base. Finally, home.

Sɪɴᴄᴇ 1894, Moody Publishers has been dedicated to equip and motivate people to advance the cause of Christ by publishing evangelical Christian literature and other media for all ages, around the world. Because we are a ministry of the Moody Bible Institute of Chicago, a portion of the proceeds from the sale of this book go to train the next generation of Christian leaders.

If we may serve you in any way in your spiritual journey toward understanding Christ and the Christian life, please contact us at www.moodypublishers.com.

"All Scripture is God-breathed and is useful for teaching, rebuking, correcting and training in righteousness, so that the man of God may be thoroughly equipped for every good work."
—2 TIMOTHY 3:16–17

MOODY
PUBLISHERS

THE NAME YOU CAN TRUST

A Savior Worth Having

ISBN: 0-8024-3132-1

If you don't know Him, you should, and you can.

Of all the names on earth today, one name is more powerful than any
other. Christians know it has the power to change lives, save lost
souls, heal sick bodies, and secure eternity. It is the name of our
beloved Savior Jesus Christ.

A *Savior Worth Having* is a collection of sermons that E.V. Hill has de-
livered over the years that all center on our wonderful Savior, Jesus
Christ. In an easy-to-read and easy-to-understand way,
E.V. Hill paints an amazing picture of our glorious Lord.

MOODY
PUBLISHERS
THE NAME YOU CAN TRUST.

1-800-678-6928 www.MoodyPublishers.com

VICTORY IN JESUS TEAM

ACQUIRING EDITOR:
Greg Thornton

COPY EDITOR:
Julie Allyson-Ieron, Joy Media

BACK COVER COPY:
Julie Allyson-Ieron, Joy Media

COVER DESIGN:
Smartt Guys Design

INTERIOR DESIGN:
Ragont Design

PRINTING AND BINDING:
Quebecor World Book Services

The typeface for the text of this book is
AGaramond